Pagan Portals

The Temple Priestesses
of Antiquity

Pagan Portals

The Temple Priestesses of Antiquity

Lady Haight-Ashton

MOON
BOOKS
Winchester, UK
Washington, USA

JOHN HUNT PUBLISHING

First published by Moon Books, 2022
Moon Books is an imprint of John Hunt Publishing Ltd., No. 3 East Street, Alresford
Hampshire SO24 9EE, UK
office@jhpbooks.net
www.johnhuntpublishing.com
www.moon-books.net

For distributor details and how to order please visit the 'Ordering' section on our website.

ISBN: 978 1 80341 028 9
978 1 80341 029 6 (ebook)
Library of Congress Control Number: 2021944122

A CIP catalogue record for this book is available from the British Library.

Design: Matthew Greenfield

UK: Printed and bound by CPI Group (UK) Ltd, Croydon, CR0 4YY
Printed in North America by CPI GPS partners

We operate a distinctive and ethical publishing philosophy in all areas of our business, from our global network of authors to production and worldwide distribution.

Contents

I dedicate this book to my loving husband, Iain Haight-Ashton, who encouraged me daily to write this book and made sure that I always had an ample supply of fine chocolate. For, you see, we Witches love our chocolate! And of course, to my three Manx cats (my familiars) Fiona, Gavan and Nessy who always sat either in my lap or nearby as I wrote.

Foreword

In *The Temple Priestesses of Antiquity* Lady shares an important narrative that needs to be heard. Many books have been written about Oracles and Sibyls but no author has had the passion or personal knowledge that Lady, as a Medium and Oracle, presents with this book. Often the psychic work of women was thought of as non-existent. With Lady's research she brings to light the profound value of these ancient Priestesses whose work saved the world. This same power exists today. Today around the globe science is looking closely at the abilities of the human brain in particular to the psychic ways we receive information. Only an Oracle could bring to life the importance of the ancient Oracles now known as Goddesses.

Laurie Cabot, HPS

Preface

I am a modern Oracle and Sibyl. I do not live in a temple complex or underground cavern, instead I have a Coven and I teach and work within the confines of my historic 18th century home in a little village in Maine. Do I predict profound prophecies or have vivid visons, or writhe in a euphoric spellbound state? Well, not exactly. Within the broad definitions of a clairvoyant, I am considered claircognizant, which means I have "a knowing". I am very good at predicting dates and affairs of the heart.

I truly believe everyone is born with the same instinctual abilities. What troubles most is "fear of the unknown" or "what we cannot explain". Trusting and letting go, allowing yourself to channel information is not easy.

Beyond the simple psychic sciences, I am also a trance psychic or medium. Yes, I can tap into the other side. In this state I am often veiled to completely block out the physical so that I can concentrate totally on the spiritual messages from beyond. (Like the Pythia Priestesses of Delphi, Greece and the Vestal Virgins of Rome).

As a Sacred Dancer I join the spirits of my ancestral sister Priestesses in mesmerizing dance movements during processional ceremonies. I am sometimes transported into their realms where I can feel their breath on my cheek and their graceful steps in time to mine.

The Ancient Temple Priestesses of Antiquity held many mysterious talents and they were so sought after that everyone from royalty to the common pilgrim came to them for oracular messages. To those of the ancient world the Oracles and Sibyls were never wrong. Our ancestors believed that these special women held a power to channel both Divinity and the ancestral dead. Their messages were never doubted. These ancient Priestesses lived a cloistered life, I do not. I am just like everyone else in the sense that I shop in stores, love to cook and entertain, clean my house and take care of three spoiled Manx cats and my loving husband. I just happen to have a unique talent and a slightly different spiritualty. I am a Witch and though one would think all Witches are either Psychics, Oracles or Sibyls, you would be very wrong. And not all Psychics are Witches either. The inner spiritual skill that many of us possess is very separate from being identified as a Witch. I consider myself blessed to have the multifaceted skills of a "seer" and the spirituality of a Witch.

The Temple Priestesses of Antiquity is a story of the women, dear to my heart, who traveled a similar road, some well-known and others forgotten to the centuries. These Priestesses lived in such different times, but one common thread was and is a devotion to our chosen Goddess. My ancestral Priestess sisters called to me again and again and thus this book is a testament to their stories and their lasting effect on the societies in which they lived.

Blessings,

Lady Haight-Ashton
Priestess of the Goddesses Lilith, Selket, Hecate and Isis

Introduction

Whether Oracles, Seers, Psychics and Sibyls, or Sacred Dancers and Healers, the ancient Temple Priestesses wove a narrative of both realism and mythology. They held court in every ancient civilization with their mysterious and mystical powers. These empowered women enthralled those who sought their advice while always serving the Goddess they revered.

Often chosen from the ranks of royalty, nobility or the politically elite, these Priestesses brought a valuable prestige and esteem to their families, as it was an honor to offer a daughter to serve Divinity. Ancient Temple Priestesses were the earthy representatives of the Goddess. Their importance transcended the ordinary because of their connection to the Divine. The Priestesses held great spiritual responsibility. The sustenance, prosperity and protection of the land was dependent upon their appropriate behavior and absolute acceptance of the rules of the Temple. Finally, many scholars and herstorians now agree that they were the anchors for the community and their success insured the well-being of all who they served.

Was it the sacred call of the Goddess that brought these women to the temple life? Was it for family honor and prestige, or political gain? Most Priestesses were chosen from royal or wealthy freeborn families. These young candidates, oftentimes around the age of puberty, also had to be physically sound, mentally stable and of course chaste, with exemplary moral character. Then began their life without the constraints of marriage and children. Temple Priestesses were independent and in many cases they could even own property. However, their duties to the Goddess and the temple superseded all else. For their service to Divinity, as Oracles and Sibyls, ritual dancers, keepers of sacred flames and sacred wells, temple housekeepers and even sometimes sacred prostitutes, they received great status and were revered. Perhaps, as many historians now acknowledge, it was a rather a good life.

As herstorians and historians recount there were strict rules of conduct and when any rules were broken severe punishments were dispersed. After all the Temple Priestess held the mystical ability to channel the Goddesses and Gods, and making these deities happy was vital. If there was even a simple misstep Divinity had to be appeased with the Priestess' punishment. Nonetheless, temple life still had significant appeal.

Being part of such a spiritual community required not only self-discipline but a deep connection with the sacrosanct. Whether voluntarily motivated or chosen by family, these women left behind all normal aspects of existence for a life of contemplative service to their Deity.

Their part in the story of the ancient world is captivating to many and inconsequential to others. Throughout the millennium historians have written and discussed the value of the Priest caste while too often only giving minimal reference to the Priestess and her contribution. These women helped shape the narrative of the ancient world with their presence.

Reading between the lines what emerges is a story no longer shrouded by interpretation. It is a story of self-lessness and piety. Ancient art on vessels and friezes have left us with a vision of women both mystifying and ethereal. It is an image that can only be defined as fascinating.

What was the real archetype of the ancient Temple Priestess? Did she feel a deep connection to the sacred? Perhaps in her role as a Temple Priestess she was a woman who felt a oneness with other spiritual realms. I believe she would have been drawn to her culture's theology with a profound interest in expanding her mystical awareness. The sanctity of her role would have given her solace in her choice of a monastic life. Yet, there were numerous instances when she might not have chosen this life for herself. I often wonder was she destined for such a life at birth or was it chosen for her for reasons of family honor, prestige or political gain? Then I wonder what type of woman would voluntarily choose this type of life for herself. Nonetheless when she was part of temple life would she have adapted to such a life of holiness and duty? Yes, I believe she would and if she had extrasensory or clairvoyant skills all the better to serve her Deity and her community. Because of her connection to the Divine, she was above the world in which she existed.

With the seclusion of temple life, she was far removed from the normal day to day activities of the time. Depending on her status within the temple community and her proficiencies she would have had a well-planned daily schedule. Some Priestess Oracles followed a strict regime for a limited number of days each month with a cycle of meditation, contemplation and ritual bathing all in preparation for their anticipated oracular messages. The Temple Priestess of antiquity was not only spiritual but also enigmatic. She cannot be easily defined.

I oftentimes marvel at the life of a modern cloistered Catholic Nun in this fast paced technically driven society. These women seem to resemble the Temple Priestesses in that their lives are so simple and precise with each minute of one's day accounted for in the service of Divinity. It is the ultimate offering up of one's individual personality for the combined good of the community. There is a parallel between a cloistered Nun and the Temple Priestess.

Could service to Divinity in a modern cloistered convent or ancient temple have heralded an awakening that conjured up in the devotee the driving force of total commitment? There is a mystery woven around the contemplative life. When a woman chooses to spend her whole life within the walls of a monastic temple or cavernous underground shrine, is her life really solitary? Perhaps the cloistered existence allows for the transcendence of the unconscious and conscious mind. Within this concept, does deity reveal hidden knowledge to the devoted

Priestess? Is there a Divine purpose that connects these secluded women to each other and to an intimacy with Deity? Is there a paradox here in the fact that the largeness of the earth did not exist within the temple walls or even now in a cloistered convent? The domain of the Priestess or Nun moves away from the expansiveness of the outside world to greet the space within one's own insightful thoughts. It is here that the Temple Priestess' story veers dramatically from that of the Nun because the Priestess' sacred concentration produced her prophetically reflective words.

Beyond the repertoire of her oracular verses, the Temple Priestess was proficient in the ritual of spiritual rites. Ancient ceremonies were magnificent holy pageants. Priestesses cascaded in spiraling processions becoming an inspiration to the neophytes and pilgrims who traveled far and wide to experience their celestial manifestation whether as a prophet or as a sacred dancer.

The remains of many ancient temple structures still exist today from the Magnificent Temple of Hathor in Dendera, Egypt to the ruins at Delphi in Greece that housed the famed Pythia Priestess. Throughout the millennium, many of these important ancient temple sites were destroyed during times of religious upheaval or were simply abandoned when religious tides turned and ultimately left to deteriorate. The sites of numerous temples of antiquity now house churches and mosques. A good example is the Temple of Artemis at Ephesus that now is the site of a pagan temple, the Basilica of St. John and the Isa Bey Mosque. With only a column still visible of the original site, it is nevertheless a very spiritually important location.

Outside the remains of above ground temple structures so familiar to historians, lay the mysterious subterranean tunnels where many ancient Oracles and Sibyls summoned the spirits of the dead. Carefully chosen pilgrims traversed the stifling deep hot labyrinths truly thinking that indeed they were traveling

14

down to Hades to speak to their ancestors through the Oracle. Many of these underground tunnels were lost to time, only to be re-discovered nearly 100 years ago. The narrative of the Oracles and Sibyls of the Dead remains divided between reality and mythos.

We know from Delphi and other ancient temple sites that Priestesses sometimes channeled their messages within a sacred space often recessed into the earth. But these were above ground temple complexes with one sacred niched area set aside for the Oracles to receive and give out their messages. The legend of "The Oracles of the Dead" is that of deep underground caverns with mazes of tunnels that went deeper and deeper into the earth until finally reaching the encompassed opening where one would meet the Oracle within her sacred space. She would physically writhe and spew out her oracular phrases to a mesmerized patron who truly believed they had entered the realm of the dead. It was here they believed the Oracle spoke to their ancestors. Unlike their sister Priestesses who lived in plush temple complexes these Priestesses lived and worked deep in the inner recesses of the earth. The demand on Oracles in the ancient world was great because no one, whether royalty or common folk, would make a decision without observing the omens interpretated by an Oracle.

Beyond the spiritual calling of the Priestesses (and the Priests), temples were a profitable business that offered solace for a price and answers to weary seekers who had expectations of an audience with an Oracle or Sibyl. Whether with generous donations or outright payments, the desperate sought answers and these prophetesses held the ancient world in their grasp.

Let us now discover within these pages the alluring story of the Priestess and her temple home whether an above ground structure or a below ground cavern shrine; her sacrosanct visions and verse; her enigmatic life; her mystifying dance and her dedication to the Goddess. She was in service not only to her chosen Divinity but to the religious culture of the time and the community thereof. She was a powerful spiritual servant who shared an extraordinary intimacy with the mysterious unknown. These prophetic women were possessors of Divine inspiration who held the key to observe and interpret omens. History weaves almost a myth around these women, but within each legend lies a reality.

So, what were the forces behind the creation of the reverent structure of temple life whether above and below ground? Could it have been something more complex than our simple understanding of fortune telling. Beginning as Matriarchal societies that transitioned into the Patriarchal, temple structure suddenly relegated the Priestess to a secondary position. Early archeologists saw the male Priests being the primary residents within temples. Fortunately, more and more archeological facts are beginning to surface, portraying the Priestess as more significant than previously interpreted. We are at the dawn of acknowledging the magnitude of the Priestesses role in ancient religious beliefs.

With the emerging story of the allusive Priestesses before us, we can now become travelers through the herstory of antiquity.

Chapter 1

The Temple Priestesses

Tales about ancient Priestesses and the Sacred Temples where they lived, received messages, prayed and worked thousands of years ago, have fascinated archeologists and historians for hundreds of years. Though some historical chronicles are still lacking in praise for these Priestesses, modern thought has now come full circle. There is an intellectual emergence happening that has welcomed a much clearer understanding of the significance of their oracular messages. With this turning tide some scholars are viewing the Temple Priestesses as the true spiritual leaders of ancient societies.

Were these ancient Oracles and Sibyls really that unique? Why is it possible for some individuals to foretell the future and to receive messages from beyond? The answer lies within our bodies control center, the human brain. It is here on the right side of our brains that we feel sensations, emotions and have the ability to perceive. It is the right hemisphere that allows us to process dreams and unspoken thought. Research has shown that most people naturally gravitate to one side of the brain over the other. Those using the left-brain hemisphere are more linear thinkers. The Temple Priestesses naturally embraced the right brain which would help to explain their amazing perceptive abilities.

It is well documented that they were sought after by patrons from the ranks of royalty, political leaders, the influential and wealthy, and even desperate pilgrims. They used their unique and otherworldly abilities whether in a dramatic trance state or within mesmerizing processional dances, to weave a spellbinding moment as they received their prophetic messages from Divinity and the dead. Did they also have important roles in ancient rituals and celebrations? We know that the Goddess Hathor's Priestesses were very desirable as ceremonial sacred dancers and musicians. Perhaps the lives of these Priestesses were more multifaceted than we have yet discovered. They weren't just Oracles or Sibyl's. They lived a deeply spiritual existence that encompassed a reclusive lifestyle. Whether guarding the sacred fires or participating in important rituals and ceremonies their lives cannot be easily defined.

Regretfully, recorded history has so often turned away from the lives of Priestesses. The focus, until recently, has been on the roles of the male Priests who were considered to be the noteworthy leaders with power and influence over the inhabitants of ancient cultures. History told of the value bestowed on the Priests by religious societies, undermining the true importance of the Priestesses. The focus has now shifted. These women were enormously essential to the ancient cultures well-being as Oracles, Sibyls, healers, sacred dancers, mystics and prophets.

There is now an awakening that recognizes the enormity of the matriarchal contribution. More and more researchers, herstorians and archeologists are beginning to recognize not only the existence but the significance of the Temple Priestesses. There is a new appreciation of the psychic sciences and the Priestesses role in offering comfort and security to ancient civilizations with their profound prophetic announcements. Priestesses were the vehicle by which the Deities could speak the truth.

Priestesses lived in complex temple structures above ground and cavernous tunnels underground. They shared vows of chastity and lived a dutiful and respected life. Temples became places where people could nourish their faith and find spiritual and religious comfort.

There arc many terms that define Oracles and Sibyls. Many scholars consider them different from each other. As a Priestess myself who does psychic work, I believe Oracles and Sibyls speak

11

the same language of prophetic messages and visions sent from the Divine or in many instances from the dead. Each Priestess was unique in her technique and abilities. Some had visions, others practiced trance mediumship or meditation, many scried into crystals, mirrors or bowls of water while others were simply clairvoyants, who just know.

What is the dictionary definition of an Oracle? Mirriam Webster's definition is:

a person (such as a Priestess of ancient Greece) through whom a deity is believed to speak the prophecies of the Delphic oracle"; a shrine in which a deity reveals hidden knowledge or the divine purpose through such a person", an answer or decision given by an oracle.[1]

And then we have the definition in Britannica:

Oracle, (Latin *oraculum* from *orare*, "to pray," or "to speak"), divine communication delivered in response to a petitioner's request; also, the seat of prophecy itself. Oracles were a branch of divination but differed from the casual pronouncements of augurs by being associated with a definite person or place.[2]

Oracles were considered to be the most important and direct means of access to Divinities revelations. The "oracles" are primarily prophetic utterances, but their narrative takes many forms from written pronouncements in various forms of prose to visions. There have been many female Oracles in the ancient world, some known and others more obscure.

Oracles in the formal sense were generally confined to the classical world. The Egyptians, however, divined from the motion of images paraded through the streets, and the Hebrews from sacred objects and dreams. Babylonian temple prophetesses also interpreted dreams. In Italy the lot oracle of Fortuna Primigenia at Praeneste was consulted even by the Roman emperors. The goddess Albunea possessed a dream oracle at Tibur (Tivoli), and the incubation rites of the god Faunus resembled those of the Greek hero Amphiaraus.[3]

The sibyls were female prophets or oracles in Ancient Greece. The earliest sibyls, according to legend, prophesied at holy sites. Their prophecies were influenced by divine inspiration from a deity; originally at Delphi and Pessinos. In Late Antiquity, various writers attested to the existence of sibyls in Greece, Italy, the Levant, and Asia Minor.[4]

Sibyls also called Sibyllas were considered prophetesses usually represented as an older woman in her crone years who uttered predications in an ecstatic frenzy. There were many known Sibylla's in the ancient world. The name Sibyl was considered a title and as more and more people wanted to know the future their popularity grew. By the late 4th century their numbers had multiplied.

In a legend about the sibyl of Cumae in Italy, she accompanied Aeneas on his journey to the Underworld (Virgil's *Aeneid*, Book VI). According to Dionysius of Halicarnassus, a famous collection of sibylline prophecies, the Sibylline Books, was offered for sale to Tarquinius Superbus, the last of the seven kings of Rome, by the Cumaean sibyl. He refused to pay her price, so the sibyl burned six of the books before finally selling him the remaining three at the price she had originally asked for all nine. The books were thereafter kept in the Temple of Jupiter on the Capitoline Hill, to be consulted only in emergencies. They were destroyed in the fire of 83 BCE.[5]

Judaean or Babylonian sibyl was credited with writing the

13

Judeo-Christian Sibylline Oracles of which 14 books survive. The sibyl came thus to be regarded by some Christians as a prophetic authority comparable to the Old Testament. On the ceiling of the Sistine Chapel, Michelangelo alternated sibyls and prophets. In the medieval hymn *Dies Irae*, the sibyl is the equal of David as a prophet.[6]

The medieval Byzantine encyclopedia, the *Suda*, credits the Hebrew Sibyl as the author of the Sibylline oracles, a collection of texts of c. the 2nd to 4th century which were collected in the 6th century.[7]

Though the Delphic Oracle and the Temple to Apollo was in Greece, there is a mythological story about a Persian Sibyl. She was known as the Babylonian, Hebrew or Egyptian Sibyl and she at one time presided over the Apollonian Oracle. She is credited as having three names: Sambethe, Helrea and Sabbe.

There were many Sibyls in the ancient world, but the Persian Sibyl allegedly foretold the exploits of Alexander of Macedon. Nicanor, who wrote a life of Alexander, mentions her.[8]

The role of Oracles and Sibyls were often interchanged in ancient historical texts. Either way both were consulted in most life situations. These Priestesses had a direct line to the Gods and Goddesses and whatever came from their lips was never questioned. Their answers determined the fate of wars, affairs of the heart and anything else.

Some temple complexes were like small cities housing many Priestesses and Priests plus their servants, creating enormous households that needed money to operate effectively. Thus, temple life became a vast money-making venture selling everything from souvenirs and mini shrines to oracular messages. All the while favoring the wealthy who could afford the fees.

There are many dictionary meanings to define a Priestess, but they all seem to use similar verbiage. She is a woman, a leader who is authorized to perform the sacred rites of a religion. She serves the needs of the spiritual community.

Each generation of Priestess was distinctively individual. Herstory records that many of the Prophetesses of the ancient world were said to speak in rhyme and deliver their oracular messages in song or written verse, hymns or in poetic form. These collections of divine revelations would then be passed down through the community moving from reality to myth and legend.

Many ancient records also reveal their exceptional stories through descriptive artwork on vessels, walls and tablets of every sort. The message is clear, Priestesses held esteemed positions in the worship and understanding of Divinity in ancient civilizations.

But what of their personalities, their needs and desires beyond that of their temple duties? Living in a communal setting is not easy as one navigates through the varied personalities that made up the inhabitants of temple life. Human nature's opposing traits such as ambition and humbleness would oftentimes appear to upset the balance within the communal setting. Yet, there must have been a devoted collective consciousness that enabled Priestesses to effectively enter into their prophetic trance states and give their oracular messages. This consciousness would have also allowed Priestesses to spiral through ritual processions in perfectly choreographed sacred dances as sister Priestesses accompanied each step with trance like rhythms on sistrums, tambourines and drums.

Women did not hold very much power in these ancient times unless you were of royal lineage, became a Queen, Princess or a Priestess. The Egyptian Queen Cleopatra was a Priestess to both the Goddesses Isis and Hathor. And there was Queen Hatshepsut, who herself held the most powerful role in Egypt, as High Priestess and thus was considered the Sun god Amun's wife. Both

Queens were politically ambitious and regretfully held the reins of power only temporarily. History tells their stories in terms of bad press. Despite what history records, herstory records that the mighty cult of the Priestess continued on.

An ancient Temple Priestess dedicated her life to beauty and the spirit of all life. She knew how to attune to the sacred energies of the universe as she performed divinely inspired ceremonies and rituals. She was an Oracle or Sibyl, poet and healer who moved with the grace of a sacred dancer. Her every action was in honor of the Goddess, the Great Mother. Her spiritual power illuminated her mystical practices for she was (and is still in the modern world) an emissary of the Divine Feminine here on earth. The position of Priestess in antiquity cannot be denied. As more and more research surfaces, it is becoming clear to many that the office of Priestess was held in great esteem, which was a blessing and a curse. For thousands of years, she held court with her holiness and her celestial messages. They were poised as leaders, teachers, counselors and inspirations. Then with the sudden shift from matriarchal societies to the patriarchal, there arose a growing fear of the Priestess and her exceptional powers. Many researchers believe that there is another answer to this shift beyond the well-known Christian takeover. There was a transference of rule that came about with the construction of towns and cities and the inevitable competition and power struggles that ensued. Slowly the role of women was regulated to a lessor position. The peace and harmony of the matriarchal culture was replaced with the more aggressive patriarchal testosterone.

Sadly, many ancient Priestesses fell prey to these drastic changes in civilization. Many felt survival in this shifting world meant denying their abilities and morphing into a Christian Nun's persona to be tucked away in a cloistered monastery. Others who held fast to their spiritual beliefs were persecuted along with midwives, healers, Pagans, Witches and Druids as the burning times crept upon the world.

The Druid Priestesses of the Goddess Brigid transformed into the Nuns of St. Bridgid in Kildare, Ireland which is said to be the first nunnery in Ireland. Brigid's sacred well is in a stone grotto in Clare, Ireland and one of the oldest wells to have healing powers. The Goddess Brigid is a triple Goddess who symbolizes higher ground, higher learning and higher consciousness. As a Triple Goddess she also represents the maiden, mother and the crone. As the patron Goddess of the Druids, she is still honored in ritual and ceremonies by her Priestesses today.

The temple honoring the Goddess Athena housed many Priestesses. Athena was the patron of Athens, Greece and her Priestesses offered a powerful presence on her behalf, in the welfare of the city. The Goddess morphed into the virginal Saint Athena who was martyred along with 40 other virgins (perhaps Priestesses) including one named Aphrodite! The Divine Feminine becomes altered into the patriarchally appointed Saint.

Another woman, whom I believe possessed a Priestess persona, was Jeanne d'Arc. Her prophetic visions and almost supernatural powers led to the liberation of France in 1430. Sadly, her magnetic leadership and her divine visions became interpretated negatively by anxious clergy hierarchy who were threatened by her strong appeal. What followed was persecution by both church and state in her Inquisitorial trial, and her ultimate execution. It is no surprise that she is eventually redeemed by being made into a Christian Saint.

Even today in many areas of the world, there is still an endless campaign of harassment and persecution against the power of the Divine Feminine. Yet people are undaunted and more than ever seek out answers from female healers, psychics and mediums.

These ancient women were elevated by their Priestess status, abandoning their personal identity in order to exemplify a larger power. They were part of a devotional community of sisters who sang and danced in religious ecstasy to rhythms that effected the human body and the psyche. What a sacred visual they must have made! For special ceremonies and ritual occasions, Priestesses wore special ornate headdresses, flowing costumes and precious jewelry as they journeyed with the Celestial. After many thousands of years of continuous dedication, the communal worship within the temples was sadly replaced with Christian church buildings.

Traveling through the millenniums research reveals stories of well-known Temple Priestesses and those that history has all but forgotten. Here lies herstory, individual and extraordinary with accounts of feminine empowerment and valued prominence in an age when women were all too often relegated to the shadows.

And what of the Priestesses who were the "Oracles of the Dead"? Living in underground caverns their approach to prophecy was very different from their above ground sisters. Sitting within subterranean fissures where toxic gasses escaped, guided by the ancestors of their patrons, words and phrases emitted from their mouths in a dramatic pageant to answer the requested questions. Where they really voices of the Dead, and channels to Divinity?

The legends and realities that become the stories of these ancient Temple Priestesses are as varied and complex as they are riveting. As an observer of herstory I am beguiled by their devotion and their longevity because they are still with us today. It is not necessary to live in a temple or a cavern to be a modern Priestess, yet we are as devoted as our ancestral sisters were to the traditions of the Oracles and Sibyls. We honor the Matriarchal Goddess in all her forms as we move forward in this ever-changing world.

Endnotes:

1.   Oracle | Definition of Oracle by Merriam-Webster (merriam-webster.com)

2. www.brittannica.com//topic/oracle-religion
3. https://www.britannica.com/topic/oracle-religion
4. https://en.wikipedia.org/wiki/Sibyl
5. https://www.britannica.com/topic/Sibyl-Greek-legendary-figure
6. https://www.britannica.com/topic/Sibyl-Greek-legendary-figure
7. https://en.wikipedia.org//wiki/Persian_Sibyl
8 https://en.wikipedia.org//wiki/Persian_Sibyl

Chapter 2

In the Beginning

Mesopotamia and the first Priestess

Early Mesopotamian civilizations began to form around 12,000 BCE, the time of the Neolithic Revolution. Some of the major Mesopotamian civilizations include the Sumerian, Assyrian, Akkadian, and Babylonian civilizations.[1]

In many ancient cultures Priests and Priestesses were considered equals. In Mesopotamian society for example the Priests and Priestesses held the same power and honor as the king and were thought to be the intermediaries between Divinity and the people. As in many ancient societies each temple was dedicated to a main Deity, who was also the central God or Goddess of the city. The temple was the home of the honored deity and thus became a sacred household.

> They were built with kitchens, tables (in the form of altars), living rooms, and the most important of the rooms, an inner sanctuary where a statue of the major deity stood in one of the building's walls.[2]

Thus, the Priestesses main role was to not only please the Gods/ Goddesses, but to decipher their will and convey those words to the sovereign and the community. Perhaps their oracular words came to them in trance or spontaneously as a hallucination or feeling. Though I prefer to move away from certain topics, it was oftentimes recorded that animal entrails were used as a sort of divination tool. Whatever the means, these Priestesses were thought to have the power to interpret these celestial messages.

The Sumerian civilization with the records dating between 4500 and 4000BC had a well-documented religious temple society. The Sumerian Temple Priestesses served Inanna who was the Goddess of "love, sexuality, prostitution and war."[3]

Sumerian Priestesses were also important in a different way:

Deified kings may have re-enacted the marriage of Inanna and Dumuzid with Priestesses.[4]

In Sumerian mythology, Dumuzid also known as Tammuz is an ancient Mesopotamian God and the primary consort of the Goddess Inanna. Thus, we have the sacred marriage which shows how integral the Priestesses role was in enacting this vital and powerful ritual.

The most famous Sumerian Priestess in the Mesopotamian region was the first known chronicled Priestess and poet Enheduanna. She was the first author in the world known by name because she was the first to actually sign her name to her work. Though there were other instances of written works well before Enheduanna's time, she was unique in that she took credit for being the author with her own signature.

She was the High Priestess of the goddess Inanna and the moon god Nanna (Sin). She lived in the Sumerian city-state of Ur.[5]

Later, Nanna/Sin would be identified as the Sumerian Goddess Inanna, the Akkadian Goddess Ishtar and, still later, as the Greek Goddess Aphrodite.

As a devoted and talented Priestess, she composed personal prayers to her Goddess. They were known as the Sumerian Temple Hymns that were carved onto 37 tablets amounting to 42 translated hymns. It was in 1927 that the British archaeologist Sir Leonard Woolley first discovered the Enheduanna calcite disc in excavations of the Sumerian city of Ur. Sir Wooley recorded his discoveries in a volume entitled *Excavations at Ur*. As the High Priestess of the Temple of Sumer, Enheduanna lived in approximately 2285-2250 BCE and was the daughter of Sargon of Akkad, also known as Sargon the Great, and Queen Tashlultum who might also have been a Priestess.

With the political intrigue of the tumultuous times in which she lived, her influence as poet and Priestess was significant. Religion played a very necessary role in the society, as did the deities themselves. Yet she was able to compose 42 hymns that addressed the temple at "Sumer and Akkad including Eridu, Sippar and Esnunna."[6]

Her hymns were copied by scribes for at least five centuries, and her writings are believed to have influenced the merger of the Sumerian Inanna with the Akkadian Ishtar. After her death, a hymn was devoted to her by an anonymous composer, indicating that she may even have been venerated as a deity herself.[7]

Enheduanna being the first Mesopotamian Princess to serve as a Temple High Priestess, she set in motion a long tradition of royalty serving the Goddess. It was the shrewd political ambitions of her father, King Sargon, to secure power in the south that prompted his appointing her as High Priestess of the City of Ur, her birthplace. She held the office for over 40 years. It was said that during the reign of her brother there was a coup and she was thrown out. Mythology records that with the help of the Goddess Inanna (Nanna), whom she served, she was restored to her proper place in the temple.

From historic records, it would seem that Enheduanna was the first woman to serve such a prominent position in Ur. This not only elevated the status of Nanna but also set an example for future priestesses.[8]

Ultimately Enheduanna had the task to combine the two deities of Inanna and Nanna into a single, omnipotent Goddess, which she did through her devotional hymns. According to historian Paul Kriwaczek:

Enheduanna is credited with creating the paradigms of poetry, psalms, and prayers used throughout the ancient world... Her compositions, though only rediscovered in modern times, remained models of petitionary prayer for even longer. Through the Babylonians, they influenced and inspired the prayers and psalms of the Hebrew Bible and the Homeric hymns of Greece. Through them, faint echoes of Enheduanna, the first named literary author in history, can even be heard in the hymnody of the early Christian church.[9]

In ancient Mesopotamia many Priestesses were Oracles or visionaries of a sort because they were thought to be adept at interpreting prophetic signs and omens. They were also known as healers. Enheduanna in her official Priestess role was more of an administrator who took care of the day- to- day temple business. But as High Priestess she would also have been required to officiate at various religious ceremonies.

Although shrouded in the mists of an ancient culture, Enheduanna's importance is likely to rise in stature. She is, after all, probably the world's oldest known author as well as a figure who evidences a significant role of women in the history of literature.[10]

Her amazing contributions to Sumerian literature are still recognized by scholars today.

Your great deeds are unparalleled; your magnificence is praised! Young woman, Inana, your praise is sweet![11]

Lines 272-274 of the translated Hymn to Inanna, a 274-line devotional hymn to Inanna as the "Lady of the Great Heart."

Other ranks of priestesses are known, most of them to be considered orders of nuns. The best-known are the votaries of the sun god, who lived in a cloister (gagûm) in Sippar. Whether, besides nuns, there were also priestesses devoted to sacred prostitution is a moot question; what is clear is that prostitutes were under the special protection of the goddess Inanna (Ishtar)[12]

Sacred prostitution was and is a subject of controversary that I will address again. Historical research does acknowledge the possible reality of such an idea which does appear in a number of ancient Temple Priestess cults.

Mesopotamian Priestesses had varied spiritual duties and responsibilities. In exchange for their valued service, they received respect, esteem and a comfortable life. Since religion and the service to Deity was so integral to the well-being of the society, each city was organized around a temple complex. There were many private chambers for the Priestesses plus work and public areas. Temple buildings were almost small cities functioning as a complex network of religious activity. Those who lived and worked within its walls were not just devoted to religious service, but to the prosperous function of the temple and all of its assets. So, each temple had many servants to help manage land holdings, tend to the crops and animals plus weave cloth all in an effort to create a functioning enterprise. In many instances the temple employed many of the city's inhabitants.

Temples employed accountants, scribes, guards, butchers,

messengers, artisans and seamstresses. Temples cared for orphans and charity wards; they also held numerous slaves who worked in a variety of capacities.[13]

There were purification rites and other sacred duties for both the Priests and Priestesses to perform. For temple life to function effectively and sometimes even as a profitable commercial enterprise, many servants (both slaves and paid workers) were employed. In many instances temples were usually the local landowners and employers. Even in the ancient world, religion was so often a business. Though we are focusing specifically on the role of the Priestesses, in Egypt the Priests sold spells and prayers to help the deceased in their journey into the underworld. It was a very lucrative business. And in many ancient temple complexes religious souvenirs in the likeness of a deity along with little altar shrines were sold to weary pilgrims.

In Mesopotamian society the temples had two overseers to supervise the scores of Priests and Priestesses. One Priest or Priestess had the responsibility of managing all sacred and religious duties including purifications and exorcisms. Another supervised the Oracles or Sibyls who understood the Divine will of the Gods and were able to communicate these messages to the ruler and to the people.

Priestesses also sang, danced and played musical instruments during religious ceremonies and in the case of Enheduanna wrote sacred hymns all in the honor of their Deity.

Perfect bodies and impressive lineage seem to have been important requirements for acceptance into a Mesopotamian temple as it was throughout the ancient world of religious sanctuaries. Training was demanding and challenging, and in many societies took many years. But the rewards were plentiful.

Priestesses served as the first dentists and doctors in Mesopotamia. They treated their patients in the temple's outer court. Priestesses were required to be celibate. Although they could not bear children, they could marry and be stepmother to their husband's children.[14]

The Priestesses of the Goddess Ishtar

Ishtar is the Akkadian name for the Sumerian Goddess Inanna. Ishtar was also associated with the Semitic Goddess Astarte. She was both a Goddess of fertility and war. The ancient Babylonian empire and the cities of Uruk and Nineveh built many grand temples and altars in her honor. Archeologists have discovered many inscriptions and art objects that attest to her popularity. There is not much known about her Priestesses but as with most Priestesses of the ancient world they were virginal and not permitted to marry.

Ishtar was sometimes described as the daughter of the Moon Goddess, Ningal, and her consort, Sin, another Moon God. Together with the Moon God, Sin and the Sun God, Shamash, Ishtar is the third figure in a triad personifying the moon, the sun, and the earth.

This powerful Mesopotamian goddess is the first known deity for which we have written evidence.[15]

Ishtar's Priestesses would honor her with incantations and singing hymns. Invoking Ishtar/Inanna was a celebration for the Goddess and was a powerful force within Sumerian culture. The ancient Priestess Enheduanna's wrote 42 personal temple hymns to the Goddess in veneration of her. Called Ishtaritu, these Priestesses specialized in the arts of dancing, music, and singing as they served in Ishtar's temples.

The Ishtar Gate was constructed by (575 BCE by order of King Nebuchadnezzar) as the eighth gate to the inner city of Babylon which is in the present day city of Hillah, Babil Governorate, Iraq. The mammoth structure was constructed to honor the

Goddess. The Pergamon Museum in Berlin, Germany created a partial reconstruction of a small frontal segment of the gate, which is now on display.

The Minoan Snake Goddess and her Priestesses

In the Middle East and parts of Asia, the Bronze Age lasted from roughly 3300 to 1200 BCE, ending abruptly with the near-simultaneous collapse of several prominent Bronze Age civilizations.

The Minoan's Era of Crete was a Bronze age civilization from 2000 BCE until 800 BCE. The ancient Minoan religion is still very much an enigma. Their language remains untranslatable, thus without any clear readable written texts from the period archaeologists and scholars have had to focus on excavated paintings, statuettes, ritual vessels, seals and rings for guidance in telling the story of this mysterious society. Yet it has been difficult to differentiate between depictions of worshippers, Priests or Priestesses, rulers and Deities. It is plausible to say that humans represented Deity in rituals which would then be reflected in Minoan art, adding to confusion in the interpretation.

Abundant amounts of statuettes of Priestesses in very elaborate ritual attire have been unearthed at Cretan archaeological sites. With almost every figurine the Priestess (or perhaps Goddess) is holding a wiggling snake in each hand. If one looks at the expression in the large and ornately painted eyes of these faces, it becomes obvious that these women were in a definite trancelike state. She is a provocative image.

In some of the temple rooms of the sprawling building found in Knossos, there were also snake pits. In small doses snake venom is a hallucinogen. Clearly these priestesses were engaging with the snake and her medicine to receive oracular information.[16]

Were these statuettes representations of "snake Priestesses"? Did snakes speak to them giving prophetic information that they would share with the community?

In Minoan Crete, they believed they were speaking literally to the snake goddess in these communions.[17]

Historians concur that the dominant figure in Minoan religion was a Goddess. It is also agreed that there was a male figure (a worshiper) often associated with the Goddess.

She seems to have been served by priestesses, and one complicating issue is that some scholars have proposed that these imitated or performed as the deity in the course of rituals, confusing what images in Minoan art represent, for example in the case of the snake goddess figurines, at least one of which may represent "priestesses", which was Sir Arthur Evans' original thought.[18]

How important was the snake to Minoan culture? The Snake Goddess was considered the most significant deity and with her snake cult of Priestesses helped to define the religious philosophy of the civilization. The snake was thought to be one of the aspects of the Great Mother Goddess. As an underworld deity, the snake was also associated with the welfare of the Minoan household.

The first who identified this Minoan Goddess and who described her domestic and chthonic role and her cult, was A. Evans. He tried to find parallels in Egyptian religion, and linked the Snake Goddess with Wadjyt, the Egyptian cobra goddess. From his point of view the attribute of the goddess — a snake — was a form of an underworld spirit, which had domestic and a friendly significance.[19]

Direct communication with the consciousness of another species has been an accepted means of oracular trance and divination throughout the ancient world. In Minoan society did we have the snake sharing her wisdom with the Priestess so that she alone could decipher the sacred knowledge? Is that why almost every statuette unearthed is in the form of a female (Priestess) holding a wriggling snake in each hand?

In our modern world Pentecostal "snake handling" is practiced primarily in a very small area of the Appalachian region of the United States. "It is the handling of live, venomous snakes during worship and is intended as an act and expression of faith."[20]

Whether Priestesses or Goddesses, these excavated figurines with their ornate and elegant garments have become the first style icons for the ancient world. What was the meaning of such stylized women with long skirts consisting of flounced layers of multicolored cloth, decorative belt/girdles and tight vestlike garments that revealed abundant naked breasts? She is also youthful and wears a crown on her head which symbolizes her high status and her power. Shortly after the Minoan culture faded it became customary for clothing to be fashionable instead of just practical. Beauty suddenly became an accepted concept.

There is much historical controversary as to what this very specific style of clothing meant. I believe the Minoan society was totally a Goddess dominate society. These are images of women who are in charge of their bodies. The well-known Egyptian Goddess Isis gave spiritual sustenance to the Pharaohs, and on and on in many ancient cultures. Did these depictions with such ample breasts symbolize giving divine nourishment?

The debate over the meaning of the ruffled flounced skirts worn by Minoan women is also intriguing. Looms were found in Minoan palaces. Being a nautical society sails would have to be made for ships. Throughout history women were weavers so perhaps our Minoan women not only made sails but created exquisite garments for themselves as well. Or were these garments so divinely designed reserved for the Priestess class? Perhaps we will never know.

Part of the attraction of the figurines is that they can be interpreted as embodying many of the perceived, and admired, characteristics of the Minoans: their elegant, fashionable costumes, their physical gracefulness, their sensitive yet forthright personalities, their sophisticated tastes and love of luxury, their refined manners and worldly ways, their seemingly high intelligence combined with an endearing forthright innocence, and their apparent love of beauty, nature, and peace.[21]

As a seafaring culture, the dress for Minoan males was fairly light and little more than a loin cloth. With our Snake Goddess, her clothing (and that of her Priestesses) represents her status and the power that she wields. In each hand of the Snake Goddess statuettes and frescoes she is holding snakes, which represents the renewal of life.

Minoans were dominant on the sea, yet there has been no significant discovery of any kind of militaristic structures or materials on the land. Perhaps we have a divided society with the men away at sea and the women at home. If this is true Minoan women not only performed ordinary tasks but used their skills to create beauty.

What was life as a Minoan Priestess like? There is evidence that they led religious rituals and it was believed that they had close associations with the Deities. Though I am focused on the mysterious Snake Goddess, it is known that the Minoans worshipped numerous other deities. Another important feature of the Minoan culture was that Priestesses and women in general were afforded status that didn't exist in other societies of the period. They were not only respected but given positions of authority.

During the Paleolithic period archeologists discovered the statute of the what is now known as the "The Venus of Willendorf". In the Bronze age we have the "Snake Goddess" which has become the manifestation of Minoan religion, art and society. Once again all of these theories support the fact that very likely Minoan society was matriarchal with a very significant Priestess cult.

And that Priestess cult is still alive and well in the modern version of the Minoan Sisterhood of Priestesses which began in New York City in 1975 with a connection to Gardnerian Witchcraft and a strong focus on the feminine mysteries.

Endnotes:

1. https://www.khanacademy.org/humanities/world-history/world-history-beginnings/ancient-mesopotamia/a/mesopotamia-article
2. https://stmuhistorymedia.org/the-role-of-temples-in-ancient-mesopotamia-2/
3. https://slife.org/sumerian-religion
4. https://en.wikipedia.org/wiki/Sumerian-religion
5. https://en.wikipedia.org/wiki/Enheduanna
6. https://en.wikipedia.org/wiki/Enheduanna
7. https://www.newworldencyclopedia.org/entry/Enheduanna
8. https://www.ancient-origins.net/history-famous-people/enheduanna-high-priestess-moon-and-first-known-author-world-007259
9. Paul Kriwaczek, 2012, *Babylon: Mesopotamia And The Birth Of Civilization*, St. Martins Griffin
10. https://www.newworldencyclopedia.org/entry/Enheduanna
11. https://etcsl.orinst.ox.ac.uk/section4/tr4073.htm
12. https://www.britannica.com/topic/Mesopotamian-religion/Cult
13. https://www.historyonthenet.com//mesopotamian-priests-

and-priestesses
14. https://www.historyonthenet.com//mesopotamian-priests-and-priestesses
15. https://nippurretreat.com/about-us
16. https://ritualgoddess.com/priestess-diviners-of-minoan-crete/priestess-diviners-of-minoan-crete/
17. https://ritualgoddess.com/priestess-diviners-of-minoan-crete/priestess-diviners-of-minoan-crete/
18. https://en.wikipedia.org/wiki/Minoan_religion
19. https://pantheon.org/articles/m/minoan_snake_goddess.html
20. https://carm.org/other-questions/what-is-pentecostal-snake-handling
21. http://arthistoryresources.net/snakegoddess/minoanculture.html

Chapter 3

Egypt

The Cult of the Goddess Isis

The great culture of ancient Egypt flourished between 5500 BCE and 30 BCE. In ancient Egyptian mythology both male and females were considered Priests. Though there was a sexual distinction, hieroglyphs record the religious hierarchy as all Priests. Within the Egyptian mythological texts Goddesses such as Isis, the Mother of Egypt and wife of Osiris considered the first Pharaoh of Egypt; Hathor the Sky Deity who helped the deceased humans enter the Duat (afterlife) held great importance. Hathor along with her Hathoric dancer Priestesses represented "music, dance, joy, love, sexuality and maternal care."[1]

Tomb paintings show the Pharaohs being suckled from the breasts of Isis drinking in the supreme power of Divinity. Thus, the Priestess's role (as the Goddess) in ancient Egypt was not just a servant to her Divinity, but was thought to be the embodiment of the Goddess on earth. Her position within the temple hierarchy was vital. These two primeval Goddesses Isis and Hathor were all powerful and can boast Cleopatra as a devoted Priestess to both.

The Goddess Isis' Priestesses would have served her as caretakers of the temple and by playing music and singing hymns in her honor. These Egyptian Priestesses would have also taken part in rituals to ensure fertility and the well-being of the land. Many of these rituals would also honor the deceased nobility and other influential personages. Throughout the day the Egyptian Priestesses as singers, musicians, and dancers performed many different rituals at the temple and in the temple complex.

In Atlantis, priestesses of the Goddess were gathering in

circles of twelve to anchor the energy of peace and harmony. They were called the Sisterhood of the Rose. They later reemerged in ancient Egypt as priestesses of Isis, with rose being a sacred symbol of the Goddess Isis.[2]

Isis, the Goddess of Life and Magick, was the Goddess of 10,000 names and her Priestesses were among the most numerous and ancient. Egyptian mythology tells the tale of the Goddess Isis using her Magick to resurrect her beloved husband Osiris after he was killed by his brother Set. She also helped her son Horus win his battle against his uncle Set. She was clever and all powerful.

During the (Greek) Ptolemaic dynasty the Priestesses of Isis worked to spread the cult beyond Egypt and Greece into the Roman empire and turn it into one of the largest spiritual cults. Thus, of the many mysteries and religious cults in Rome, the one devoted to the Egyptian Goddess Isis was by far the most popular. It was said that it was the Goddess Isis herself who chose her Priestesses and that they were "experts in astrology, interpretation of dreams and conjuring of spirits.[3]

Isis' Priestesses practiced abstinence and worshipped their Goddess throughout the day with prayer and ritual lifting the veil to reveal the Goddess to her followers. Why was the Goddess Isis and her Priestesses not only popular, but enduring? Though I cannot prove that what I have been told is true, there were functioning temples to honor Isis all the way up to World War II.

Could it have been her connection to the Virgin Mary? Isis, the Supreme mother of the universe so often portrayed just like the Madonna with child. Isis with Horus and Mary with Jesus. Is it religious coincidence that the same divinity was transformed by hierarchy to the new religious and cultural mandate? Art through the ages beautifully illustrates Isis and Mary as eternal Mothers cradling their newborn deities. Isis tenderly holds her son Horus who she protects from Set, his evil uncle. While

Mary holds her son Jesus who she guards from King Herod. The ultimate maternal Goddesses. Images of Isis, Queen of the Heavens with stars surrounding her head like a glowing halo mimics similar images of Mary. Thus, to be a Priestess of Isis was to traverse the centuries carefully to survive and they did!

Priestesses still exist and practice within Temples and Covens today. One organization that has an international membership is The Fellowship of Isis (FOI), headquartered at Huntington (Clonegal) Castle in Ireland. The FOI is a peaceful society with members worldwide from all cultures, races and religions. The Priestesses of the FOI honor the Divine Feminine in all of Her forms and the good in all faiths. The FOI was founded on the Vernal Equinox of 1976 by Olivia Robertson and her brother Lawrence Durdin-Robertson and his wife Pamela. Since there are a growing number of people re-discovering the Goddess, the FOI has temples and devotees throughout the world. Anyone can join, as members or to enroll in the priesthood. Priestesses of Isis feel a close communion with the Goddess. For further information contact: http://fellowshipofisis.com/

Hathor, Goddess of Love and her Sacred Dancers

What is the allure for a dancer to embrace the sacred within? Is it just simply a moment in time or an experience that influences our destiny? Do the Muses push us toward our path? I believe we are all dancers in our hearts. Our bodies feel rhythms to which most of us will move our heads, others tap their feet while some of us release our inhibitions and let our bodies move in rhythmic expression. Dance movement gives us a creative connection to our inner spirit. It is liberating to our souls and healing to our mind and body. As Isadora Duncan observed, "the dancer's body is simply the luminous manifestation of the soul."

The beginnings of civilization and the evolution of communication into ritual to honor the seasons, animals, and elements brought us the earliest expression of sacred movement.

Thus, such animated movement and spontaneous dance became a necessary element in ancient rituals for Temple Priestesses who honored the highest entities, Goddess and God.

Our ancestors knew how to communicate their joys, sorrows and spiritual desires through movement. Their bodies became the best instrument with which to express their desires, needs, and prayers. Movement evolved into a language of dance for communication with the forces of nature, joining the ancients to the mysterious and awesome powers of Deity. As ritual, stylized dance became part of every religious and social occasion such as birth, death, marriage, war, victory, harvest and hunting.

Not only was dance an integral part of ritual celebration, but it also developed into one of the primary Magickal tools for healing, exorcism, obtaining fertility, protection, forgiveness, etc. In time, dance came to be the province of religious specialists – Priestess, Priest and Shaman alike.

One after the other, ancient Priestesses left their temple cloisters to dance in ritual processions moving to freely choreographed aerobic and stylized phrases while banging tambourines, cills, rattles, flutes and sistrums. The dancers' ritual energy conjured up an atmosphere of joyous festivity and magnificent pageantry. These sacrosanct visuals must have transfixed pilgrims and spellbound onlookers alike. How resplendent were these Priestesses in their flowing gossamer tunics and ornately be-ribboned hair styles? Each in blessed service to their Goddess.

Sacred, mystical or Magickal dancing are the embodiment of a powerful and focused inner spiritual motivation. To many sacred temple Priestess dancers such movements would have transported them into an inspirational meditation of motion. Sacred Ritual Dance was and still is the integration of the spirit to the mind which expresses the meditative voice within. Through dance many of the ancient Priestesses and now her modern counterparts channel the Divinity of their chosen Goddess.

Priestess dancers created a form of ritual whenever it was performed and experienced. Our ancient roots lay in the celebration of life's splendid harmony, the panorama of the seasons, the mysteries of the moon cycles, the sadness of death and the eternal joy of rebirth. The Priestesses were mesmerized within the hypnotizing trance of spiraling dance.

The great Egyptian Goddess Hathor with her Magnificent Temple in Dendera Egypt housed many Priestesses. Though they were called upon at times for their Oracle advice they were mostly known as Sacred Processional Dancers, acrobatic dancers, musicians, singers, and actors. The definition of religious worship for these Hathoric Priestess dancers was to incorporate music and dance in extravagant pageantry as acts of praise to Hathor. One musical instrument, called a sistrum, which is a rattle-like instrument, was very important in the worship of Hathor. Many statues and hieroglyphs of Hathor that archeologists have discovered show her holding a sistrum. And today many modern Priestess dancers (such as myself) dance within our ritual processions ringing the sensuous vibrations of our sistrums in her honor.

Hathor's Temple at Dendera is one of the best-preserved temples in Egypt and is a marvelous complex with intricately decorated rooms and corridors, fronted columns, crypts, chapel rooms, a birthing room and a sanctuary. Because of the archeological evidence we can clearly piece together the lives of these Dancing Priestesses whose memory still enchants.

Even within Hathor's Temple there is a structure devoted to the honor of the great Goddess Isis.

The Temple of the Goddess Isis is situated behind the main temple near the sacred pool. It is small and not as decorative...[4]

Today, at every Full Moon, as they have for thousands of years, Goddess cultures still gather to celebrate the passage of another

Moon cycle with ritual processions and spiraling dances that move to the rhythms of the Earth and Heavens.

It was in 9000-year-old cave paintings found in India, that dance was first depicted. Perhaps that is the oldest proof of the existence of dance. Dancing can be traced back to the 3rd millennia BCE, when dance became an integral part of the Egyptians religious ceremonies and rituals. Musical instruments were used by Egyptian Priests/Priestesses as dancers mimicked important events – "stories of gods and cosmic patterns of moving stars".[5]

The Egyptian Goddess Hathor among her many titles is known as the mistress of music and dance. Images of her musicians and Priestess dancers playing tambourines, harps, lyres, and sistrums all in Hathor's honor appear on numerous temple reliefs and tomb paintings. The rattle-like sistrum, so essential to Hathor's worship, has erotic implications that by extension referred to the creation of new life.

Many of Hathor's annual festivals were ritually celebrated with drinking and processional dancing by her Hathoric Priestess dancers.

> Revelers at these festivals may have aimed to reach a state of religious ecstasy, which was otherwise rare or nonexistent in ancient Egyptian religion. Graves-Brown suggests that celebrants in Hathor's festivals aimed to reach an altered state of consciousness to allow them interact with the divine realm.[6]

Hathor's Priestesses were also thought to be Prophetesses and were known as a "Prophet of Hathor."[7] And they were also known as Oracles.

> Hathor's priestesses wore patterned red dresses, long red scarves, and beaded menat necklaces.[8]

Within the Priestess cults of the Goddess Hathor there was also the ritual of weaving and the presentation of red cloth. There is an inscription at the Temple of Dendera which refers to women of the Priestess class that translates to: "She who unites with the Red Cloth".[9]

Thus, dance was a necessary part of religious ritual life in the ancient world. During the Sed-Festival and Opet Festival in Egypt processions of both female and male dancers chanted and played musical instruments.

Hathor's Priestesses who ritually danced (and even women who weren't Priestesses) wore diaphanous flowing red robes and dresses, simple belted girdles, often made of beads or cowrie shells, allowing their bodies to move about freely. One can imagine such a spectacle. Sensuous dancing Priestesses moving in elaborate choreographed incense filled processions while musicians, also Priestesses, played rhythmic melodies on sistrums and drums creating an atmosphere of otherworldliness for all those who watched. The Priestesses would have seemed to the onlooker as being in a trance like state within the ritual moment. A text from the Temple of Edfu says of Hathor: "...the gods play the sistrum for her, the goddesses dance for her to dispel her bad temper."[10]

The act of shaking a sistrum was also thought to protect the goddess and her subjects. This protection is made clear by scenes at the Temple of Hathor at Dendera that are captioned:
"I have taken the Seshseshet sistrum,
I grasp the sistrum and drive away the one who is hostile to Hathor, Mistress of Heaven
I dispel what is evil by means of the sistrum in my hand."[11]

Though it has not been proven definitively there were women of this era who wore very detailed tattoos. Archeologists have excavated various female mummies and this has sparked a controversary about whether these tattooed mummies were Priestesses of Hathor or not. The most famous of these tattooed mummies is Amunet, Priestess of the Goddess Hathor.

Amunet's tattoos were located on her superior pubic region covering the lower part of her abdomen, on her mid frontal torso and directly inferior to her right breast. She also has tattoos superior to her elbow joint and on her left shoulder as well as on her thighs. Most of these tattoos are in the form of dashes, and dots and some form concentric circles on her abdomen.[12]

Many historians have dismissed these tattooed Priestesses as women of low status, prostitutes, royal concubines or dancing girls. However, they were found in Deir el-Bahari a royal and high-status burial site. Even before the discovery of these mummies, we still had clear evidence that Egyptians were tattooed from burial tomb paintings and artifacts. Perhaps the meaning behind these tattoo's is something altogether different. Are they evidence that our ancestors had a more high-level awareness of healing with acupressure and neural pathways in a person's body? Were the Priestesses administering a form of pain supervision? It is interesting to note that though male and female mummies are discovered in tombs, it was only females who were tattooed. The birth of children was vital to the success of all ancient civilizations, as it is today in our modern world. Is it possible that these tattoos on female bodies were meant to protect and assist women in this dangerous process? Are these examples of medical tattoos?

Previously tiny faience female figurines showing tattoo patterns on their thighs, wrists, abdomen, and upper body had been discovered in tombs and the tattoos on the newly discovered mummies were in many instances almost identical to the figurines.[13]

Suddenly it became obvious that the tiny figurines were actually depicting real tattoos and their meanings could be directly traced to the priestesses of Hathor.[14]

Some scholars believe that these figurines were fertility charms or amulets for the deceased to help guide them on their journey. Or did they represent Hathor herself as the Lady of the West who welcomes the deceased to the underworld? There are prejudices in the academic community when the role of the Priestess and her influence on society is discussed. But to myself and many other "herstorians" the role of the Priestess was not only meaningful but immensely formidable.

It is agreed though, that within the Temple walls Hathor's Priestesses held an equal position to that of the male Priests. A rather unique concept during a time when women were considered inconsequential in many ways. Beyond being categorized as "Hathoric Dancers", it is also plausible that they held medical knowledge that would have given them legitimate power in their own right.

Nubian women appear in Egyptian tomb and temple paintings as dancers for the goddess Hathor from the Middle Kingdom (2100-1900 BCE) through the Roman period (30 BCE-395 CE). These women performed wearing brightly colored leather skirts, cowrie shell belts, and displaying tattoos on their breasts, abdomens, and thighs. Recently, several tattooed, mummified female bodies have been excavated from the C-Group Nubian cemetery at Hierakonpolis, in Egypt. The dot and dash, lozenge-shaped tattoos found on those women are very similar to tattoos found on contemporaneous priestesses of Hathor buried at the royal funerary complex of the Middle Kingdom ruler, Mentuhotep II (2061-2010 BCE).[15]

Part of the initiation of a Priestess in Hator's cult required a ritual known as "The Five Gifts of Hathor" in which the initiate would be asked to name five things that they were most grateful for while looking at the fingers of their left hand. It became a very important responsibility for a Priestess of Hathor to understand the importance of gratitude in their spiritual life. This ceremonial tradition was handed down orally and became a part of the daily life of each Priestess.

By naming the five things one was grateful for, and identifying them with the fingers of the left hand, one was constantly reminded of the good things in one's life and this kept one from the 'gateway sin' of ingratitude from which, it was thought, all other sins followed. For the more affluent of Egypt, considering the Five Gifts would have been a way to keep from envying those more prosperous than oneself and a means by which one was reminded to be humble in the face of the gods.[16]

Endnotes:

1. https://en.wikipedia.org/wiki/Hathor
2. www.thegoldenagegoddess.com/p/the-sisterhood-of-rose-network-of.html
3. https://templeofisispompeii.weebly.com/the-cult-of-isis.html
4. https://www.atlasobscura.com/places/hathor-temple
5. http://www.dancefacts.net/dance-history/history-of-dance/
6. https://en.wikipedia.org/wiki/Hathor
7. https://www.everythingselectric.com/hathor-priestesses/
8. https://www.everythingselectric.com/hathor-priestesses/
9. Women in Religion in Ancient Egypt/Per Ankh https://www.everythingselectric.com/
10. https://en.wikipedia.org//wiki/Hathor
11. https://www.hathorsystrum.com//about-the-systrum/musician-priestesses
12. https://www.ancient-origins.net/myths-legends/tattooed-priestesses-hathor-001122
13. https://www.ancient-origins.net/myths-legends/tattooed-priestesses-hathor-001122
14. https://www.ancient-origins.net/myths-legends/tattooed-priestesses-hathor-001122
15. https://www.arce.org/event/dancing-hathor-nubian-women-priestesses
16. https://www.ancient.eu/Hathor/

Chapter 4

The Greco-Roman World

Priestess Eumachia

The societies of ancient Greece span a timeframe from approximately 800 BCE to around 146 BCE. Let us begin with the Temple of Isis at Pompeii and the Priestess Eumachia who was part of the Isis cult in Pompeii that was thought to arrive there around 100 BCE. Though the cult of Isis originated in ancient Egypt, her recognition spread extensively throughout the Greco-Roman world.

> Eumachia is important as an example of how a Roman woman of non-imperial/non-aristocratic descent could become an important figure in a community and involved in public affairs. She is seen as representative for the increasing involvement of women in politics, using the power of a public priestess, the only political office able to be held by a woman for social mobility.[1]

In ancient Greece as in other ancient societies Priestesses played an important part in the well-being of the populace. Greek societies worshipped a number of Gods/Goddesses. I like to focus on the more relevant deities and their Temple Priestesses.

Priestesses of the Goddesses Artemis and Diana of Ephesus

The Temple of Artemis in Ephesus Greece was also known as the Temple of Diana. The Greek Artemis morphed into the Roman Goddess Diana as both were virginal Goddesses of the Hunt and the Moon. Their temple at Ephesus was completely rebuilt three times though the millennium and parts of its rebuilt structure still stands today.

Artemis' shrines, temples and festivals (*Artemisia*) could be found throughout the Greek world, but the Ephesian Temple to Artemis was unique because it was once considered one of the Seven Wonders of the World. Mythology tells us that the Goddess Diana was born in the woods near Ephesus, where her temple was built.

Also, according to tradition, the city which was later called Ephesus was founded by the Amazons, and Diana or Cybele was the deity of those half-mythical people.[2]

Thus far, there is no clear evidence of this fact. The priestesses of Ephesus were so numerous, that they were commonly called Melissai or bees. Coins in Ephesus were struck with the symbol of bees.

The Melissai, which in the early times were all virgins, were of three classes; it is no longer known just what the special duties of each class were. The ritual of the temple services consisted of sacrifices and of ceremonial prostitution, a practice which was common to many of the religions of the ancient Orient, and which still exists among some of the obscure tribes of Asia Minor.[3]

The Goddesses Artemis and Diana represent the wildness of nature. Artemis is oftentimes shown as a powerful presence standing with a bow and arrow next to her dog. As Artemis of Ephesus, she was also the protector of women in childbirth and fertility and with that persona she is often portrayed as a woman with multiple breasts signifying the mother of all life. Artemis was considered a virgin and was also the Goddess of wild animals, childbirth and vegetation.

The similar virginal Diana, it was said, was a huntress and

also portrayed as an archer. Diana was one of three Goddesses, which includes Vesta and Minerva, who had sworn to honor their virginal vow not to marry.

During festivals and ritual processions ancient Priestesses of both Artemis and Diana danced passionately and lasciviously as maidens representing tree nymphs (dryads) honoring the woodland natures of their Divinities.

These chaste Goddesses required their Priestesses to be virginal also. They were most likely chosen from rich aristocratic Ephesian families who paid for the privilege of having their daughters serve in this way as a sort of rite of passage or perhaps to honor their households. Since the mythology of Ephesus included the theory that the fierce female dominated tribe of the Amazonians may have founded the city, this Matriarchal superiority may have been deeply engrained in its culture.

With the popularity of these Goddesses growing, vast numbers of little shrines honoring both Artemis and Diana, made of clay or marble, have been unearthed in many archeological sites.

They are exceedingly crude; in a little shell-like bit of clay, a crude clay female figure sits, sometimes with a tambourine in one hand and a cup in the other, or with a lion at her side or beneath her foot.[4]

These shrines were vastly popular with traveling pilgrims. Though it is recorded that the male Priests were selling these simple shrines to pilgrims on their journey, I believe that the Priestesses of the Temple would have also been taking part in this revenue venture.

It seems that the Ephesian Priestesses and the female identity of the Ephesians portrayed women as empowered and very capable. Diana and Artemis were powerful Goddesses defenders of Ephesus along with their strong Priestesses.

Her character and function varied greatly from place to place, but, apparently, behind all forms lay the goddess of wild nature, who danced, usually accompanied by nymphs, in mountains, forests, and marshes.[5]

Artemis supervised waters and lush wild growth, attended by nymphs of wells and springs (naiads). In parts of the peninsula her dances were wild and lascivious.[6]

The Goddess Athena, patron of Athens and her Priestesses

In ancient Athens there was a large complex of temples honoring Athena: the Parthenon; Erechtheion; Old Temple of Athena; Sanctuary of Pandrosos; Temple of Athena Nike and Temple of Zeus and Athena. As with our Goddesses and Priestesses of Diana and Artemis of Ephesus, Athena was a warrior Goddess. She was the patron Goddess of Athens and her High Priestess held the most important religious position in Athens. Coming from a noble family of the "Eteoboutadae"[7] she would have exerted considerable influence both religiously and politically. All the Priestesses in Athens played vital roles in the religious and civic duties of Athena's cult.

The Holy Priestesses of Ancient Athens, also known as Jediis, were given the divine role to protect the home of the mother Goddess Athena. They also protected the fountain of youth from invaders (that legend states was there). All of the original women who bore the name of the Athenian Priestesses were regarded with such reverence that they were almost Saints in their own right.

There was no mortal owner of the Temple to Athena as it was the property of the Mother Goddess Pallas Athena. The monastery within the temple was run by the Priestesses who showed absolute abstinence from the outside world. Athena's Priestesses were the caretakers of all life, the spreaders of pure love and in charge of all the food and water that went in and out of the temple.

Just like the Vestal Virgins of Rome, the Priestesses of Greek religious temples enjoyed many perks that other Greek women were not privy to. In exchange for their service and commitment they were often paid, given property and were respected. As celebrities they were considered role models.

Athens celebrated Panathenaea, Athena's birthday, every year with great festivities. Every fourth year Athens celebrated the greater Panathenaea which was an even more splendid festival and included the Panathenaic Procession.

> In preparation for the procession to the Acropolis, a new peplos, or robe, was made for the cult statue of Athena that was housed on the acropolis. Two young girls from noble families were chosen by the Archon Basileus as *arrephoroi*, to live with the Priestesses of Athena for a period of time and help to weave the new garment.[8]

The well-known Parthenon frieze shows the dancing Priestesses of the Panathenaic Procession. It confirms that while the average woman of Athens was not appreciated, those in religious service such as the Priestesses were revered and "were able to break down barriers and contribute publicly in the arenas of politics, civics, and religion."[9]

The High Priestess of the Goddess Athena Polias (the protective deity of Ancient Athens) was regarded as the highest religious office in Athens and she would have enjoyed prodigious stature and influence. She not only managed the cult of Athena but was the superior of the minor officers. She was granted supreme power over the temple at Athens and she was the leading resource of direct communication with the Mother Goddess Athena. In addition, there was a High Priestess of Poseidon-Erecheteus and a Priestess of Athena Nike. These composed the three important cults to the Goddess Athena in

Ancient Athens.

Only the virgin Priestesses were allowed to enter the holy of holies and speak directly to the Mother Goddess Athena. These Priestesses were knowledgeable in all of the spiritual rites and showed an extraordinary degree of selflessness, dedication and self-sacrifice in service to Athena.

Endnotes:

1. https://en.wikipedia.org//wiki/Eumachia#
2. https://www.biblestudytools.com/encyclopedias/isbe/diana-artemis.html
3. https://www.biblestudytools.com/encyclopedias/isbe/diana-artemis.html
4. https://www.biblestudytools.com/encyclopedias/isbe/diana-artemis.html
5. https://www.britannica.com/topic/Artemis-Greek-goddess
6. https://www.britannica.com/topic/Artemis-Greek-goddess
7. https://brewminate.com/-the-cult-of-athena-in-ancient-greece/
8. https://brewminate.com/-the-cult-of-athena-in-ancient-greece/
9. https://brewminate.com/-the-cult-of-athena-in-ancient-greece/

Chapter 5

The Delphic Oracle

Out of all the many Temple Priestesses of antiquity more is known about the multidimensional Pythia Priestess of Delphi, than any other.

Delphi the center (or navel) of the world to the Greeks and known as the Omphalos of Delphi was the seat of the famous Pythia Priestess Oracle. Originally Delphi was a Priestess cult to honor the Goddess Gaia, the Mother Goddess of Greek mythology. As herstory gave way to history, the cult of Gaia and the Pythia Priestesses morphed into the cult and Temple of Apollo.

Today the temple ruins at Delphi still occupy an imposing place on the south-western slope of Mount Parnassus, over-looking the coastal plain to the south and the valley of Phocis.

The mythology (or reality) of the Pythia of Delphi is thought to be older and more commanding than the classical Olympic gods, including Zeus and Apollo. It is said that the Pythia's prophecies began long before the Greek gods were even born.

Mythology tells us that the Mother Goddess Gaia gave birth to other children before the Olympic gods, including Python which is represented in Greek mythology as the largest snake in the world and the original Oracle at Delphi. Python was said to have inherited all Gaia's wisdom and knowledge. As guardian and protector of her sacred city of Krisa, he sent prophecies to his Oracle Priestess Pythia and inspired her mystical visions. It is said that the Pythia sat atop a gilded tripod over the underground chasm breathing in the sacred pneuma (fumes that rose directly from Python's decaying body to inspire her visions.)

In earlier myths before the temple honored Gaia solely it was also possessed by the Goddesses Themis and Phoebe. Themis was the Greek Goddess of Law and Order and was closely linked to the oracles. The Goddess Phoebe was the sister of Themis and the Titan Goddess of prophetic radiance.

Though history records very little about the actual workings and rituals at Delphi, sources do describe the Pythia Priestess delivering prophecies (some easily interpreted while others considered gibberish) while in a profound trance under the influence of vapors and fumes that rose from a chasm in the Adyton, the inner sanctum of the oracle.

The intimate chamber allowed the escaping vapors to be contained in quarters close enough to provoke intoxicating effects. Plutarch reports that the temple was filled with a sweet smell when the "deity" was present:[1]

Plutarch (46 CE – died after 119 CE) was a Greek Middle Platonist philosopher, historian, biographer, essayist and priest at the Temple of Apollo where he spent the last thirty years of his life. He observed first-hand the process of receiving oracle prophesies.

In *On the Cessation of Oracles* Plutarch records a number of oracles from the Pythia's and also describes in the form of a diary or journal the personalities and lives the Priestesses. "There is no umbril of the land or sea: God only knows, man knows not, if there be" an Oracle recorded by Plutarch to have been spoken by a Pythia Priestess. His interpretation is as follows:

With good cause, therefore, did the god repulse him when he was testing the ancient story, like some old painting, by the touch.[2]

Mythology states that during the 11th to the 9th century BCE a new god, honored by the patriarchal priests, named Apollo, seized the temple from Gaia. The great emphasis that was placed upon the Pythia Priestess' chastity was then re-interpretated and ultimately reserved for her union with the God Apollo (similar to the chaste Catholic Nuns of today who wear a golden wedding band symbolizing that they are brides of Christ).

From that time forward, once a month, the Oracle would undergo purification rites meant to ritually prepare her for communication with the Divine. Then on the seventh day of each month (which was sacred to Apollo), with a purple veil covering her face she was attended by two oracular male Priests as one would pronounce the following:

Servant of the Delphian Apollo
Go to the Castalian Spring
Wash in its silvery eddies,
And return cleansed to the temple.
Guard your lips from offence
To those who ask for oracles.
Let the God's answer come
Pure from all private fault.[3]

During the next part of the ritual the naked Pythia bathed in the Castalian Spring and then drank the holy waters of the Cassotis that flowed near the temple. Here it was said a naiad (a type of female spirit) who possessed magical powers lived. Then escorted by oracular servants and followers carrying laurel branches (sacred to Apollo) the Pythia's procession went upward along the pathway of the winding Sacred Way. Then removing her veil, to reveal a short white robe, the Pythia mounted her tripod seat, holding laurel leaves and a dish of Cassotis spring water into which she gazed.

Nearby was the omphalos (Greek for "navel"), which was flanked by two solid gold eagles representing the authority of Zeus, and the cleft from which emerged the sacred pneuma."

Ancient sources describe the priestess using "laurel" to inspire her prophecies. Several alternative plant candidates have been suggested including Cannabis, Hyoscyamus, Rhododendron and Oleander. [4]

Oleander is another possible hallucinogenic because it causes signs similar to those shown by the Pythia in her seizures. Research states that the Pythia would burn oleander leaves and inhale the smoke. The epileptic seizures that she experienced were thought to be a "sacred disease" can come from the toxic substances of oleander. Could this have been interpretated as the Pythia being possessed by the spirit of the Goddess Gaia, or the Python, and in later years the God Apollo? Plutarch serving as a priest at Delphi reported that the

oracle of Delphi usually seemed as though she had run a race or danced an ecstatic dance. According to him, she sometimes flung herself around and raved in a delirious state.[5]

Researchers and archeologists agree that the temple sat over a point where two fissures in the earth cross each other. Ground analysis below the temple denotes the presence of ethylene, a sweet-smelling gas which could have flowed to the surface, resulting in a hallucinogenic delirium and ecstasy. Once she was fully immersed in a state of divine frenzy, flinging herself around and raving in a state of delirium, the Pythia would channel the God Apollo. History credits her prophecies as messages from Apollo whilst herstory attributes the Pythia's communications to her own particular prophetic abilities.

Because the popularity of the Pythia's oracles was very sought after, the average petitioner drew lots to determine the order of their admission. As with most religious cultures, those high-ranking individuals who were willing to pay could jump ahead.

Plutarch describes the events of one session in which the omens were ill-favored, but the Oracle was consulted nonetheless. The priests proceeded to receive the prophecy, but the result was a hysterical uncontrollable reaction from the priestess that resulted in her death a few days later.[6]

Those pilgrims and supplicants who journeyed far and wide to seek the advice of the Oracle were called consultants (those who seek counsel). These consultants were interviewed by attending male Priests before being allowed to be presented to the Oracle. Part of the journey would be watching processions along the Sacred Way with dancing Priestesses carrying laurel leaves enticing and enchanting worthy supplicants, with an ethereal vision.

Finally, the seeker would be led into the temple to enter the Adyton (the innermost sanctuary shrine) to present their gifts to the Oracle and ask their carefully framed question of the Pythia to receive an answer. With all of the pious ritual preparation the supplicant would surely have been aroused into a devout meditative state.

Though there is little substantial evidence, it was said that when the Pythia was not available, a consultant could obtain guidance by simply asking a yes or no question from a Temple Priestess who would toss colored beans, one color designating yes and the other no.

There is much controversary about the validity of the Pythia's utterances.

Although the seer may have at times been incoherent due to various intoxicants, some say the prophecies she uttered were often deliberately ambiguous. Lack of clarity and detail helped to preserve the authority of the oracle; it might be better to be vague than to be outright wrong. This strategy may have kept the Oracle at Delphi in high esteem for many years.[7]

With all of the theories that abound about just how the Pythia went into trance, there is yet another regarding the bite of a snake and the effects of its venom. This mimics the Christian snake handlers of today who believe that numerous snake bites make them immune and bring on mystical visions.

> When people immunized against snake-bite are bitten by a venomous snake (particularly by a krait, cobra, or another elapid), they experience an emotional and mental state that has been compared to the effects of hallucinogenic substances.[8]

Thus, I do not agree with the theory (and so-called evidence) that the priests of Apollo dictated to the Pythia. Another theory is discussed in the book, *Sibyls,* by Jorge Guillermo, where there are continuous references to sacrifice. History states that no female prophet could possibly go into trance, or predict anything without a sacrifice! From my research I believe that is history. I ascribe to "herstory".

> It wasn't until the late 1980s and 1990s that a team of geologists, archaeologists, forensic chemists, and toxicologists re-examined the site and discovered that the Temple at Delphi not only has various fissures, but is in fact located precisely at the intersection to two crossing seismic fault lines, one running east-west, the other north-south.[9]

Perhaps it was between these two fault lines that the sweet-smelling ethylene that seeped through the fissures only to be breathed in by the Pythia as she entered the Adyton that helped to create her sacred visions and connection to the Divine. Since there is no definitive answer to the Pythia's remarkable inspiration, other than many varied and valid possibilities, will we ever know for sure? Recently I read that traces of ethylene had been found in the waters of the Castalian spring which is now part of the modern town of Delphi's water supply!

Picture the sought-after Pythia Priestess sitting upon her tripod perforated with holes as she inhales the mysterious vapors. As with any hallucinogenic one's complexion would change, heart begin to pound as the breast swells. Her voice would have seemed to mimic an other-worldly presence. Those watching would have been mesmerized at such a mystical sight. Her utterances would have transcended earthly words to become those of prophetic sanctity.

Of the few spoken oracles of Delphi known to have survived since classical times, history records over half are said to be accurate historically.

And what of the famous phrase "know thyself" found inscribed at the entrance to the Temple? Phenome was a poet in Greek mythology and was said to be a daughter of Apollo and his first Priestess at Delphi and the inventor of the hexameter verses, a type of poetic metre. Some researches attribute the phrase "know thyself" to her.

> Inscribed on a column in the pronaos (forecourt) of the temple were an enigmatic "E" and three maxims:
> Know thyself
> Nothing to excess
> Surety brings ruin, or "make a pledge and mischief is nigh"[10]

History and legend states that the Oracle only gave prophecies during the nine warmest months of the year because Apollo deserted his temple during the wintry months. His place was taken by his divine half-brother Dionysus. We do not have any clear records that state the oracle participated in the Dionysian rites of the Maenads, but "Plutarch informs us that his friend Clea was both a Priestess to Apollo and to the sacred rites of Dionysus". [11]

Upon the death of her predecessor, a new Pythia was

chosen from amongst the Priestesses of the Temple. As with other religious cultures women who were chosen to become Priestesses where required to have both good character and good health. Usually coming from affluent and noble families, they were expected to be well-educated in the important topics of the day such as geography, politics, history, philosophy and the arts. Though some candidates for Priestess were married, upon entering the temple, all outside relations ceased.

Did the Priestesses really speak their oracular messages in hexameters or pentameters or were these words interpretated and transcribed by Priests? This notion is still up for debate because history doesn't seem able to give that credit to the Priestesses. In later years these oracular messages were composed more in a prose style rather than in hexameter. Perhaps because the stringent rules for choosing a Priestess became more relaxed and having well educated Priestesses was not as important as those with the right prophetic abilities. Their aptitude in being able to speak to Divinity was foremost.

Being the Pythia or a Priestess was not only a respectable calling but one that brought the rewards of liberties such as "freedom from taxation, the right to own property and attend public events, a salary and housing provided by the state, a wide range of duties depending on their affiliation, and often gold crowns.[12]

There were other officiants besides the Priestesses at the Temple in Delphi. Plutarch, who gave us a window into the lives of the Priestesses and especially the Pythia's, was a Priest there. At any given time, there were two male Priests in attendance. But it was the Pythia Priestesses who held court.

The Greeks as with many other societies believed in the practice of consulting oracles and considered them the human voices of the Gods in their perpetual need to receive divine guidance and divine approval.

The last recorded oracle was in 393AD when by order of Emperor Theodosius I the temple was closed and never reopened. The Oracle declared *all is ended*. Within 5 years the Emperor was dead and 15 years later Alaric and the Visigoths captured Rome.[13]

Thus, it was said that the last Roman reached out to the last oracle but learned nothing to comfort him, nothing to inspire, nothing to suggest that the gods foresaw a bright future. Instead, the Pythia's reply began a long silence.

Tell the king, the fair-wrought house has fallen
No shelter has Apollo, nor sacred laurel leaves;
The fountains now are silent, the voice is stilled.
The Delphic Oracle, 393 AD

Endnotes:
1. https://en.wikipedia.org/wiki/Pythia
2. Page 2 "On the Cessation of Oracles" by Plutarch (anonymously printed in Middleton, DE 04 February 2019).
3. https://en.wikipedia.org/wiki/Pythia
4. https://en.wikipedia.org/wiki/Delphi
5. https://en.wikipedia.org/wiki/Delphi
6. https://en.wikipedia.org/wiki/Pythia
7. https://www.historicmysteries.com/oracle-of-delphi-pythia/
8. serpentsanctum.com/pythia-oracle-of-delphi
9. serpentsanctum.com/pythia-oracle-of-delphi
10. https://en.wikipedia.org./wiki/Pythia
11. https://www.newworldencyclopedia.org./entry/Pythia
12. https://300.fandom.com/wiki/Pythia
13. https://en.wikipedia.org/wiki/List_of_oracular_statements_from_Delphi

Chapter 6

Sacred Wives and Virgins

Aphrodite and her sister Venus

Aphrodite was the Greek Goddess of love, beauty, pleasure, passion and procreation. Her Roman Goddess Sister Venus and her share the symbols of myrtles, roses, doves, sparrows and swans. Her Priestesses lived in temples in Cythera, Cyprus, Corinth and Athens. Aphrodisia was her special festival celebrated in her honor by her Priestesses annually in midsummer. Aphrodite had temples throughout Greece and the Temple of Venus and Roma was thought to have been the largest temple in Ancient Rome. Most captivating is the thought that Aphrodite was considered the patron of prostitutes.

Scholars in the nineteenth and twentieth centuries believed that the cult of Aphrodite may have involved ritual prostitution, an assumption based on ambiguous passages in certain ancient texts, particularly a fragment of a *skolion* by the Boeotia poet Pindar, which mentions prostitutes in Corinth in association with Aphrodite. Modern scholars now dismiss the notion of ritual prostitution in Greece as a "historiographic myth" with no factual basis.[1]

There were many temples to Aphrodite in the city of Corinth in south central Greece, the Temple at Acrocorinth, Temple of Aphrodite II, and others at Kraneion, Leachaion and Cenchreae. The Temple at Acrocorinth built in the 5th century BCE was the most famous. Among the ruins are a few columns of the original sanctuary venerating Aphrodite which are still standing.

Temple of Aphrodite at Acrocorinth is above all famous for

the claims of the temple prostitution of courtesans, which were said to be dedicated to the service of the temple, and contributed to the attraction of visitors to the city of Corinth.[2]

Many Priestesses in Goddess cults were thought to be virgins. In the ancient Pagan and Goddess traditions the term "virgin" simply meant a woman who is not beholden to any man and free to love as she chooses.

Did cult or sacred prostitution really exist in the ancient world? It was normal practice for all Priestesses to channel the Goddess being her earthly representative of the sacrosanct. Did the ecstasy of transcendence in trance also allow the act of copulation to be Divine? Was it meant to empower a ruler, emperor or wealthy powerful politician of the time with the essence of Divinity and thus secure their godlike authority? It is likely that a Priestess had control of her choices of sexual partners with the High Priestess acting as a participant in the re-enactment of the sacred marriage between God and Goddess.

> The idea or reality of a priestess in the guise of a 'Divine Wife' or 'Sacred Prostitute' seems nothing more than the definition of an enlightened woman who embraces her spirituality within her sexuality as she channels the revered missive of the Goddess. She allows the celestial ecstasy to fill her spiritual and physical being". Within the aura of her mystical awareness, she would have become the architect of pleasure in that partnership between Feminine Divinity and man.[3]

The Vestal Virgins

The mysterious Vestal Virgins served in the temple honoring the Goddess Vesta, Goddess of the Hearth, in Rome. The name Vesta is the short Latin version of Hestia (Goddess of the Hearth) who was the daughter of the God Chronos (time) and Goddess Rhea (earth). Vesta represented the domestic hearth of the city.

As with many ancient Priestesses, the Vestals were free from the accepted social obligations of marrying and bearing children. Their story is a little more stringent because they took a 30-year vow of chastity in order to devote themselves to the study and correct observance of state rituals. They were chosen from between the ages of six and ten, had to be freeborn of respectable freeborn parents (though later the daughters of freedmen were eligible), have both parents alive, and be free from physical and mental defects.

Beginning the ceremony of initiation, a Vestal candidate's hair was closely clipped (like the Christian nuns who take the veil). The Vestal was then robed in the white costume of the Vestals and her shorn hair was bound with a white woolen riband, or fillet called a Vitta.

The title of Pontifex Maximus was given to the chief Priest in Rome, who history describes as the religious teacher and authority, the interpreter of all sacred rites, ceremonies and offerings. He was also the person who inspected the holy virgins called Vestals and monitored their lives in all aspects.

The house of the Vestal Virgins where they lived was on the Roman Forum near the Temple honoring the Goddess Vesta. There they lived a lifestyle of responsibility, and the most important duty by far was tending the perpetual fire in the Temple of Vesta. Other duties like keeping their vow of chastity, fetching water from a sacred spring (Vesta would have no water from the city water-supply system) preparing ritual food, caring for objects in the temple's inner sanctuary and officiating at the Vestalia (festival) from June 7-15, were important duties. But central and vitally important was tending to the perpetual fire. Romans believed that the chastity of the Vestals had a direct effect on the health and well-being of the state. When a Vestal entered the life of service to the Goddess Vesta, she left behind her father's authority and became a daughter of Rome.

The sacred flame, the ever giving and ever receiving fire,

held in the Holy of Holies within the Atrium was an emblem of purity. There were other things to keep in this most secret of places within the temple that were kept from the sight of all but the Vestals. Though it is said that the Pontifex Maximus actually re-kindled the sacred fire annually, it was the Vestals who not only assisted him but were required to perpetuate its flame. In addition to the various duties recorded, the Vestal Virgins were expected to attend certain annual Roman festivals that numbered at least twenty.

Much has been recorded and debated in reference to the punishment of Vestals who neglected their duties. Depending upon the offense, there might be a scourging or beating. This was carried out in the dark and through a curtain to preserve the Vestals modesty. But the most severe punishment was given when the vow of chastity was violated. History relates that this offense was punished by a live burial because the blood of a Vestal could not be spilled. Luckily there are only a few instances when this severe punishment was actually carried out. The many rules of conduct and duties performed had a specific purpose, to keep the Goddess Vesta appeased so that she would not withdraw her protection of the state.

But, for all the rigidity, the Vestal Virgins enjoyed many privileges that were not available to women in other religious cultures. And as with other Temple Priestesses, the Vestals held an important and honored social status, were completely emancipated from their families rule and in many documented cases owned and managed their own property.

Their 30 years of service was divided into three 10-year periods. The first was their time as students, during the second decade they became servants of the temple and the Goddess Vesta and during the last 10 years they finally became teachers

When the Vestal had passed all the grades as a Priestess and completed her 30 years of service, she became a High Vestal Virgin. Each Vestal would then retire to be replaced by a new initiate. And at that juncture she was given a pension and became free to take a husband. Marrying a Vestal was a very great honor and brought the spouse and his family very high-status, in addition to a good pension and good luck.

The Pontifex Maximus, acting as the father of the bride, would typically arrange a marriage with a suitable Roman nobleman.[4]

Vestal Virgins, in Roman religion, six priestesses, representing the daughters of the royal house, who tended the state cult of Vesta, the goddess of the hearth. The cult is believed to date to the 7th century BCE; like other non-Christian cults, it was banned in 394 CE by Theodosius I.[5]

The ancient historians and authors Livy, Plutarch and Aulus Gellius all agree that King Numa Pompilius, who reigned circa 717-673 BCE was the creator of the Vestals as a state-supported Priestess cult. According to Livy, King Numa presented the Vestals and apportioned salaries to them from the public treasury. The 2nd century antiquarian Aulus Gellius writes that the first Vestal taken from her parents was led away in hand by Numa. Plutarch, (philosopher, historian, biographer, essayist, and a Priest at the temple at Delphi), ascribes the founding of the Temple of Vesta to Numa, who assigned the first two priestesses.

The Temple of Vesta was thought to be a circular structure with a doomed roof. Though legend says that it might have burned to the ground more than once, there is a certainty that during the Renaissance period in 1549 CE, the temple was demolished. Its marble was repurposed to build churches and papal palaces. Most of the information we have regarding the look of the temple comes from its depictions on coins and art.

A beautiful relief of this last Temple of Vesta exists in the

Uffizi Palace at Florence. It shows the door with four columns on its right, facing toward the east, whilst it is approached by seven steps; the columns are fluted with composite capitals, peculiarly short, the lower part below the Ionic volute being composed of aloe leaves.[6]

Endnotes:

1. https://en.wikipedia.org/wiki/Aphrodite
2. https://en.wikipedia.org/wiki/Temple_of_Aphrodite_at_Acrocorinth
3. Lady Haight-Ashton, 2019, *The First Sisters: Lilith and Eve*, Pagan Portals, Moon Books, pgs. 57, 58 John Hunt Publishing
4. https://en.wikipedia.org/wiki/Vestal_Virgin
5. www.britannica.com/topic/Vestal-Virgins
6. T. Cato Worsfold, 2010, *The History of the Vestal Virgins of Rome*, Kessinger Publishing, LLC

Chapter 7

The Forgotten Oracles and Sibyl Priestesses

The Ile de Sein and the Gallizenae

One group of Oracles, not very well known, were the Gallizenae from the Ile de Sein, a French islet in the Atlantic Ocean. It has been said that the Ile de Sein has been inhabited since prehistoric times, and it was reputed to have been the very last refuge of the Druids in Brittany. Nine in number, these ancient Priestesses were said to have the power to predict the future, to control the weather by calming the winds and to become shape shifters taking the forms of different animals. Not much more is known of these elusive Priestesses, even their temple if there was one, has vanished. All that remains are a few megalithic menhirs (standing stones) to mark what possibly once was a sacred site. The writer Robert Graves states:

> ...the island was once home to a conclave of nine virgin priestesses believed to hold magical powers, who might be approached by those who sailed to consult them.[1]

According to many classical authors, the Gallizenae (or Gallisenae) were Oracles, Priestesses and/or Druidesses. The Greek geographer Artemidorus Ephesius first mentioned their existence. Later Greek historian Strabo wrote that their island was forbidden to men and that at times the women or Priestesses left the island and came to the mainland to meet their future husbands.

Ancient legends record that the Ile de Sein belonged to a Gallic divinity and was famous for its Oracle, whose Priestesses, sanctified by their perpetual virginity were nine in number.

The island women used to wear a black headdress, and in the

past, they had a reputation for enticing sailors onto the rocks by witchcraft. In the past, it was also known for its wreckers.[2]

Wreckers are persons who look out for floundering ships that run aground close to shore and seize any valuables on board. Many believed that these Priestesses used their will to raise large storms at sea around the Island. So, it makes sense that legends tell of ship navigators who travelled to the Island specifically to consult the Gallizenae about the future of their voyages and perhaps to procure their protection.

These nine Priestesses, called the Gallizenae, lived in the holiness of perpetual virginity. The French Island of Ile de Sein in the Atlantic Ocean where they lived was desolate and treeless. Since so much of their story has been lost to history, we must rely on legends and tales passed down through the ages. They were Oracles and Sibyls, seers and healers who seemed to have supernatural powers to know what was to come and how to foretell it.

It is mentioned by the Roman geographer Pomponius Mela that "there are two megalithic menhirs on the island, which is flat and treeless."[3]

Though the temple itself is gone there are a few megalithic ruins (standing stones called menhirs) of this sacred site still visible. These upright stones typically date from the European Bronze age. Though we have no clear evidence of the fact. One wonders if these menhirs are what remains of an ancient stone circle or sacred way. The island as I mentioned is treeless, resembling a large rock with the Chaussee de Sein, a vast zone of reefs that stretches for more than thirty miles from east to west that requires numerous lighthouses all in an effort to prevent shipwrecks. For in the past, there were many shipwrecks, which made the history of the island so mysterious.

Legends tell us that the Gallizenae used their magic charms to stir up the seas and winds and could cure illnesses that seemed incurable and they could predict the future.

> Isolated as they were...these stories of their "Powers" were not revealed to just anyone... only to sea-voyagers and then only to those traveling to consult them.[4]

This ancient island is also reputed to be the last place of refuge for the Druids in Brittany. Today three hundred islanders, who still make their living from the sea, reside there among its narrow-labyrinth twisted streets that protect against the violent sea winds.

Many classical authors write of these mysterious nine Priestesses as Druidesses and that their island was forbidden to men. Today some refer to the island as the Isle des Druidesses.

One of the most interesting aspects of this fascinating myth is that these nine Priestesses are somewhat intertwined with the mythology of Morgan and the Arthurian legend because of Morgan's nine sister Priestesses and the isolation and mystery of the Ile de Sein. So, can the Ile de Sein be in the mythological running as one of the possible fabled Islands of Avalon?

> Pomponius Mela was a Roman chronicler during the first century CE. He mentioned the nine priestesses of the Isle of Sena in his literary works.[5]

> Several nineteenth century folklorists noted that the motif of the Nine Maidens occurred in other places and one of these was the reference from the 2nd century Greek geographer Strabo who refers to the nine Druidesses of the Isle du Sein off Brittany who were called the Gallicenae.[6]

The nine sisters of Avalon are only one legend. We also have the nine Witches of Caer Lyow and the nine maidens of Pictish saint lore. Thus, the Gallizenae of the Ile de Sein seem to fit within these folklores very nicely. Ultimately the Christian church demonized these myths of nine magickal Priestesses and their story almost fades from history.

> The nine damsels of the cauldron recall the nine virgins of the Ile of Sein in Western Brittany in the early 5th century A.D. as described by Pomponius Mela".[7]

In the Middle Ages, the Ile de Sein became caught up in the Arthurian legends and according to some storytellers, is the birthplace of two of the most accomplished magicians, the wizard Merlin, and Morgan La Fée.[8]

There was a druid Priestess by the name of Veleda who was thought to be a Divinity on Earth. Interestingly she is sometimes associated with the Ile de Sein. Myths describe her as a Prophetess and Oracle and that she had nine sisters. It was said that she lived in a tower and refused to receive mortal supplicants but only accepted questions from messengers who were related to her. Was Veleda and her Priestesses the forerunners to the Nine Priestesses on the Ile? We may never know for sure. And there are other myths of nine priestesses such as the daughters of Zeus, and my favorites, the Muses or Fates.

Clio - History
Erato - Lyric/Erotic Poetry
Euterpe - Music
Melpomene - Tragedy
Polyhymnia - Choral Poetry
Terpsichore - Dance
Thalia - Comedy
Urania – Astronomy

The Ile de Sein was very isolated and it would have been a contemplative and lonely existence for the Priestesses who lived there. Seekers asking for prophecies, advise or protection would have come by ship over turbulent waters. I am sure that the sailors of old either felt that the nine Priestesses protected them through their Magickal chants or perhaps the total opposite... that they lured them to shipwreck. Or perhaps they charmed the winds and the waves with their songs to ensure a safe sailing though the reefs. Beyond their roles as Oracles and healers, the pre-Christian myths and legends of the Island seem to connect the Gallizenae to the Druids and their rituals. Sadly, there is not much beyond myths that is known about their everyday life, except that they depended on the donations of pilgrims.

Though we equate the menhirs, still visible on the Island, as part of whatever temple existed during the time of the Gallizenae, there are ancient Christian sanctuaries still there. One is of the Church of St. Guenole and the other the chapel of St. Corentin, which was erected at a place called *Goulénez*, (which sounds familiar to the Priestesses name). One of the island's oldest sacred places with a freshwater source. It seems that most ancient temple sites were constructed near a sacred spring or lake.

The (French) *Insight Guide* (1994), says of the island: "Bretons call Ile de Sein Enez Sun, and it is suggested that this helps to identify it as the Isle of the Dead, a burial place of the druids. It is also said to be the Romans' Insula Sena, a mysterious island where sailors used to consult an oracle tended by nine priestesses."[9]

Solitude, contemplation and psychic visions were their life. We can only imagine how they lived, since they are the some of the most elusive and mysterious Priestesses of antiquity.

Hypatia of Alexendria

Hypatia was born between 350–370 CE in Alexandria, Egypt. She was a Hellenistic Neoplatonist philosopher, astronomer and mathematician. As the librarian of the Library of Alexandria she lectured extensively to masses of loyal students and large audiences. Hypatia was not only a beautiful woman but a wise woman renowned in her lifetime as a great teacher and judicious counselor. It was a true loss to the ancient world when she was brutally murdered in 415 CE for her philosophical beliefs by a mob of Christian fanatics. Her views and principles were interpreted as pagan during a time of bitter religious conflict between Christians (both orthodox and heretical), Jews, and pagans.

Though not a clear Sibyl or Oracle, Hypatia was indeed a brilliant woman who honored the Goddess in a Priestess persona. She was a stunning woman adored by her students and a powerful feminist symbol of the time. As with our Vestal Virgins of Rome, Hypatia embraced a life of dedicated virginity. Did Hypatia hide her Priestess initiation? Many believe that she was a member of the Order of Hermes an organization that attempted to unite gifted individuals and offer a defense against hostile forces of energy.

Regretfully she was most remembered for her cruel death instead of her writings, commentaries and her true and unwavering belief in the power of the Divine Feminine.

Chrysis a High Priestess of the Goddess Hera

In ancient Greece the Priestesses (and Priests) played an important role in society. As with most ancient cultures Priestesses were virgins or at the very least beyond child bearing age. Oftentimes Priestesses and Priests were the same sex as the Deity they served. Temples and sacred sites honored the Olympian deities of Athena Apollo, Aphrodite, Ares, Artemis, Demeter, Dionysos, Hades, Hephaistos, Hermes, Poseidon and Zeus.

In order to become free of harm, ancient Greek priests and priestesses wore a sacred headband. Their main duties were to carry out religious ceremonies and prayers.[10]

These temples were places of Divine connection. Here resided the great Oracles such as those at the Temple to Gaia and then Apollo at Delphi. The centers where messages were received were vitally important, not only in Greece but all over the ancient world.

One such Greek Priestess was Chrysis a High Priestess of the Goddess Hera. She was a formidable and respected Priestess and a prominent member of the cult of Kosmos. Sadly, history only remembers her for one devasting error in judgement.

In the summer of 423 B.C., Chrysis, the priestess of Hera at Argos, fell asleep inside the goddess's great temple, and a torch she had left ablaze set fire to the sacred garlands there, burning the building to the ground.[11]

Chrysis survived the fire and fled from Argos and ultimately to the sanctuary Temple of Athena Alea where she found asylum.

Sibyl Prophetess of the Eleusinian Mysteries and the cult of Demeter

There are no clear records about the content of the secret Rites of Eleusis or the Eleusinian Mysteries. The ancient Greeks observed the mysteries regularly from circa 1600 BCE to 392 BCE, yet all we know about the rites came from the brave testimonials of the initiated. The initiates were required to swear to secrecy on pain of death that the details of the ritual will never be known.

Priestesses would not only supervise the ritual, but in all likelihood, they would have entered a trance state in order to channel the powerful spirit of Demeter or her daughter Persephone as they re-enacted the mystery. Initiates would have seen a vision of the afterlife that became a revelation that changed the way they saw the world and their place in it. In understanding the mystery, one would recognize that they are only temporarily in their mortal bodies and thus would have no fear of death.

Here lies the most famous story of Greek mythology. Persephone a beautiful young maiden is picking colorful flowers when she is spotted by Hades, the Lord of the Underworld, He is transfixed and immediately falls madly in love. He kidnaps her by pulling her down with him deep into the underground. Her mother the Goddess Demeter was so devasted at the loss of her daughter that she cries and cries and turns into a withered old woman. The plants of the earth stop growing and begin to die. Tired of hearing Demeter's unrelenting sobs, Zeus the Sky God realizing that the human race will perish, convinces Hades to allow Persephone to return to her mother. Hades agrees but first he makes Persephone taste some pomegranate seeds. Supposedly, those who taste the food of the underworld (the pomegranate) are forever bound to return there. Therefore, Persephone returns to the Earth, but she is condemned to spend three winter months in the underworld with her husband Hades each year. Every Spring she is released to come back to the earth and the plants start blooming again. The cycle continues.

The Ank Priestesses of the Isle of Iona

The mysterious sacred Isle of Iona is one of several small islands (one of the Inner Hebrides) off the western coast of Scotland.

> It's Gaelic name, Inns-nam Druid beach means 'Island of the Druids'. Forty-eight Scottish kings including Mac Beth and the Lords of the Isles are buried there.[12]

The ancient Priestesses on the Island of Iona called themselves the Priestesses of Ank which means 'sacred well of life'. The name Ank is reminiscent of the Egyptian Ankh, which means 'life'. It is said that these Priestesses used scrying, a means of prophecy and revelation, using a suitable medium such as a crystal ball or bowl of water. During this practice of divination, the Priestess would stare into the medium to receive messages or visions from the Divine.

I want to comment on the uniqueness of these Ank Priestesses. Scrying has been used throughout the ancient world up to the present day by Mediums, Psychics and Witches to foretell the future and to experience astral (out-of-body) projection. The purpose of such Divine channeling is to see oracular revelations that take the seer on a visual journey beyond the physical.

As with the Pythia Priestesses of Delphi these Priestesses of Iona would have gone into a deep trancelike state in order to open the layers of the etheric dimensions to receive their messages. These Priestesses were not exposed to underground vapors, but simply looked into their medium of scrying to receive their oracular communications.

These Priestesses of Ank welcomed certain spiritually attuned Druids and other individuals into their sacred sanctuary stronghold. Some for healing and others for learning for it was said that they understood the etheric layers of dimensions and could travel unhindered by the physical.

Mythology tells of astral initiations for these Iona Priestesses. Traveling though the astral plains within an out-of-body experience could only have been accomplished with advanced learning into the realms of deep meditation. Did some exceptional women come to the Isle, not in their physical bodies, but in an ethereal astrophysical state? Some say that there are still otherworldly presences there today.

As with the Gallisenae Priestesses from the Ile de Sein, "Arthurian legends and those of the Lady of the Lake have been linked to myths of this this small magical island.[13]

Iona shares her sacred space of ocean with several other islands, one of which is the tiny Staffa. Uninhabited today, it harbors two enormous caves, whose current names are Mackinnon's and Fingal's. In the time of the Ank priestesses of Iona, these caves were magical enclaves for their oracle use.[14]

Female Shamans

Though not considered Priestesses who once lived in ornate temple complexes, the "wise woman" female Shamans of the ancient world were at the forefront of many indigenous and tribal societies. It was believed that they had the power to heal the sick and communicate with spirits and gods. Like the Oracle Priestesses, these mysterious women entered into a state of trance through deep meditation, sacred dance and drumming, which allowed their enlightened visions and dreams to come forth. They practiced traditional folk healing and midwifery and like their sisters the Temple Priestesses were respected and served the spiritual needs of their community.

Researchers believe that Shamanism is one of the oldest divinatory practices, that possibly has existed since the beginning for over 20,000 years with accounts in almost every area of the world.

These early Female Shaman provide an unbroken lineage of Shamanic Priestesses that emerged in Crete and the Mediterranean area in the late Bronze Age but arose from the confluence of earlier streams of Woman Shamans from Africa, Europe, and Asia.[15]

Was there a golden age 10,000 years ago when the world was ruled by matriarchal societies and humanity lived in peace and harmony? Archeologists and historians believe this idea is simply a mythological vision for the feminist movement. Perhaps myths evolved from the truth of reality.

Priestesses initiates of the Goddess, were wise teachers and healers.

There is a Buddhist view that sees Priestesses as "Lightning conductors that divert human energy currents straight to the World Soul.[16]

Priestesses of the ancient Druids

There was a misconception among historians and researchers

that the intellectual elite Druids were only male. Herstory attests to the fact that there were female Druids as Priestesses. The earliest records of the Druids can be traced back to the 3rd century BCE. The Druids were not just religious leaders of the Celts but scientists, astrologers, magicians and poets. History records that to gain the necessary knowledge in alchemy it took more than 19 years. Let us remember the 30-year service of the Vestal Virgin Priestesses with their time as students, servants of the temple and finally teachers. Let us also remember Hypatia who was an intellectual, teacher mathematician, astrologer, scientist, author all-around brilliant women who honored the Goddess. So, I cannot imagine why history has such a hard time finding references to the Druid Priestess.

They worshipped the Goddess and celebrated with rituals and feasts during different months. The most important Goddess to the Celts was Brighid who was later morphed into Saint Brigid by the Christians and her Priestesses became her cloistered Nuns. Though historical texts mostly ignore the fact that the Celts had a Priestess class, archeologists have recently discovered the existence of female Druid burials in Germany dating back to the 4th century BCE. Some of them were buried with symbols of great status such as jewels and precious objects including a distinctive torque.

According to researchers, only a Druidess could have a big enough status to receive a burial like this.[17]

The Roman Gaius Julius Caesar wrote that he was aware of female Druids and the author, Strabo, wrote about a group of religious women who lived on an island near the river Loir. Tacitus, the author of *Histories*, the Roman Historical chronicles (written circa 100–110 AD), mentions female Druids living on the Island of Mona in Wales and that there was no distinction between the male and female rulers. It seems that female Druid

Priestesses did exist and were very powerful.

According to Plutarch, female Celts were nothing like Roman or Greek women. They were active in negotiating treaties and wars, and they participated in assemblies and mediated quarrels. According to the 'Pomponius Mela', virgin priestesses who could predict the future lived on the island of Sena, in Brittany.[18] This was the very island where the Gallizenae Priestesses resided.

In medieval Irish legends they were called Banduri or Bandorai. Their existence was confirmed by ancient Greek and Roman writers.[19]

Hildegard of Bingen, Visionary

Hildegard of Bingen (1098 – 17 September 1179) was not literally a Priestess, but she did live in a cloister, took a vow of chastity and was a profound Oracle. She referred to her prophetic visions as both illuminations and reflections of the living light. She was a devoted and brilliant medieval abbess from her Christian monastery in Rupersburg high on a hill in rural Germany. She was an Oracle of great depth whose visions inspired her writings as a theologian, her botanical and medicinal texts as well as hymns and poetic liturgies. Many in Europe consider her to be the founder of scientific natural history in Germany.

There are more surviving chants by Hildegard than any other composer from the entire Middle Ages, and she is one of the few known composers to have written both the music and the words.[20]

She fought the patriarchs from her cloister to be heard and she was.

Asenath wife of Joseph and the Disciple
Mary Magdalene

The illusive Asenath was an aristocratic Egyptian woman. Though Asenath is a minor figure in the Book of Genesis she remains a powerful mystery. Was she an Egyptian Priestess who was willing to convert to Judaism?

Her importance is related to the birth of her two sons, who later become forefathers of two of the twelve tribes of Israel.[21]

Some mythologies tell of the famous disciple and wife of Jesus, Mary Magdalene as a Priestess of Isis and Ishtar. The Egyptian Isis along with the Sumerian Ishtar being both profound and sacred popular Goddesses would have inspired a woman such as Mary Magdalene. As a Priestess Mary would have learned the mystical secrets that gave her the illuminating light of knowledge. And her alabaster jar of pungent and mystical oil, called the Chrism would have been used to anoint.[22]

Many researchers and herstorians feel that there is obvious and strong evidence that Mary Magdalene was a Temple Priestess. And that she was initiated into the matriarchal teachings of the Goddess. And as a Temple Priestess she would have practiced the divine rite of "sacred marriage" called "hieros gamos" bestowing the power of Divinity into those she initiated. Hieros gamos or Hierogamy is a holy or sacred marriage. Participants representing deities as Goddess and God enact the symbolic ritual. "Hieros gamos is described as the prototype of fertility rituals."[23]

Mary Magdalene was also an apostle and consort of Jesus. A Priestess/bride (Mary Magdalene) anoints the King her Bridegroom (Jesus) during the sacred marriage. Here again is her Chrism or mystical oil that we see Mary holding in her alabaster jar in many ancient paintings. In the Bible it is Mary who anoints Jesus' body before burial.

Jesus was one to unite all people, regardless of social status or religion, so a marriage entered between him and a priestess would be a symbol of the union between the Mother Goddess of the pagan, Earth-fertility religions and the Father God of the Old Testament, creating a new religion that honors and embraces both masculine and feminine energies and harnesses the creative power inherent in all people.[24]

As I have discovered in my research through the years, the title of "virgin" was often bestowed upon the Sacred Temple Priestesses in the ancient world. Was the Mother Mary part of a divine union also as a Temple Priestess whose virgin born or divine child was Jesus? There has been so very much written about both the mother Mary and Mary Magdalene that is controversial. I only want to touch on their lives in relation to their connection to the Temple Priestess.

Four pieces of Gospel evidence strongly point to Mary Magdalene as a temple priestess of the Goddess. The first is her title "Magdalene," almost identical to "Magdala," noted earlier to be the name of the triple-towered temple of the Goddess Mari-Anna-Ishtar. Literally, "Mary of the Magdala" signifies "Mary of the Goddess Temple." Christian tradition has said that Mary is of the town "Magdala" or "Migdal," which was known as "The Village of Doves," a place where sacred doves were bred for the Goddess temple. In either case, two threads of strong symbolism link the name Magdalene to contemporary Goddess worship.[25]

So, whether you believe that either of these Mary's lived part of their lives as a Temple Priestess is not the argument. Herstory does make a plausible opinion that does have relevance.

Five Worthy Sibyls

The Erythraean Sibyl was the prophetess presiding over the Apollonian Oracle at Erythrae in the Greek town of Ionia. Depictions of the Erythraea Sibyl can be seen as a floor mosaic in the Cathedral of Siena, in Italy. Her prophecies were written in the acrostic style on carefully arranged leaves so that the initial letters of the leaves always formed a word. As a Sibyl her answers were given depending on the value of the question and then were given directly. She is credited with predicting the coming of Jesus Christ (the redeemer).

> Apollodorus of Erythrae, however, says that one who was his own countrywoman predicted the Trojan War and prophesied to the Greeks both that Troy would be destroyed and that Homer would write falsehoods.[26]

The Persian Sibyl, named Sambethe, was sometimes also called the Babylonian Sibyl and was one of four Sibyl's in residence at Delphi during the 2nd century CE. Another of the four was the Hebrew Sibyl who is credited in the medieval Byzantine encyclopedia, the Suda, as the author of the Sibylline oracles. The Libyan Sibyl presided as Oracle at the Siwa Oasis in the Western Desert of Egypt and as legend relates Alexander the Great consulted her after his conquest of Egypt. The Hellespontine Sibyl, or Trojan Sibyl, presided over the Apollonian Oracle at Dardania, Greece.

The Tiburtine Sibyl by the name of Albunea, was Roman and from the ancient town of Sabino-Latin, the town of Tibur (now modern Tivoli). She was worshiped as a Goddess. There is a mythology wrapped around this Sibyl whereby the Roman Emperor, Augustus, inquired of her whether he should be worshipped as a God? In 380 CE legend says that she prophesized the advent of a final emperor by the name of Constans who would vanquish the foes of Christianity. There are many ancient fresco murals depicting this and many other events attributed to her.

The Prophecies of Ancient Witches

Witches of Isle of Mull: The Isle of Mull is the second largest of the Inner Hebrides and lies off the west coast of Scotland. There are no stories of ancient Priestesses, Temples or Oracles associated with the Isle. But there are myths and legends that tell of a group of women Witches who lived on the Isle many centuries ago and had amazing, and some say Magickal, powers. Thus, although the information about them is scant, tales of these Witches hold my interest. They were not fortunetellers but Witches who held the power of curses. Images were made of the targeted person in wax or clay, that the Witches would prick or punch. Ultimately the person would experience great suffering. But not all curses can be negative.

Local folklore says a 1558 spell cast by Mull witch Doideag caused the explosion that sank a member of the Spanish Armada in Tobermory harbour.[27]

Mother Shipton: Ursula Sontheil (c.1488-1561) popularly known as Mother Shipton, after she married Toby Shipton, was an English soothsayer and prophetess. In 1641, eighty years after her reported death an edition of her prophecies was printed. Though it contained various regional predictions and two prophetic verses it was not given much credence because it was thought to be simply a mythological account. She seemed a faerie tale personage with narratives of turning kings into stone. She was thought to be born in a cave to a 15-year named old Agatha and that Ursula was very ugly! Agatha ended up in a convent and Ursula was shuttled between foster homes.

Despite the varied fictional legends about her, she did exist and she did make predictions, told fortunes and was a popular and respected herbalist throughout her life.

The North Berwick Witches: In the 16th century a group of men and women were named the Berwick Witches. Legend or reality states that they caused a deadly storm through witchcraft to drown King James I. So often predictions are misunderstood and I believe that is what happened here. But vengeance was declared upon them by the surviving James I. They were arrested, brought to trial, tortured and burnt. This some say started the first great witch hunt in Scotland. By the 17th century Witchcraft was in full swing in Scotland. Perhaps these so called Witches were simply prophesying the future to a misguided populace.

Joan Wyttle: Joan Wyttle was born in 1775 and was a Cornish woman. Legend called her the Fighting Fairy woman of Bodmin and that she was a clairvoyant and healer. Because of an illness she became feisty and was imprisoned as a result of a fight. Regretfully she died there in 1813 and it is said she haunts the Museum of Witchcraft in Cornwall, where her unburied bones were once displayed.

Endnotes:

1. Graves, Robert (1961). *The White Goddess*. London: Faber & Faber. p. 111. ISBN 0-571-06961-4.
2. https://en.wikipedia.org/wiki/Île_de_Sein
3. Graves, Robert (1961). *The White Goddess*. London: Faber & Faber. p. 111. ISBN 0-571-06961-4
4. https://en.wikipedia.org/wiki/Île_de_Sein
5. https://legendsoflove.wordpress.com/2019/05/22/the-nine-priestesses-of-the-isle-of-sena-in-brittany
6. https://goddess-pages.co.uk/goddess-nine-maidens/
7. Graves, Robert (1961). *The White Goddess*. London: Faber & Faber. p. 111. ISBN 0-571-06961-4

8. https://thejournalofantiquities.com/2016/08/18/les-causeurs-menhirs-ile-de-sein-finistere-bretagne-brittany/
9. https://thejournalofantiquities.com/2018/04/24/st-corentins-chapel-ile-de-sein-finistere-bretagne-brittany/
10. www.ancientpages.com/2016/07/27/role-priests-priestesses-ancient-greece/
11. https://www.nytimes.com/2007/07/01/books/review/Coates-t.html
12. http://www.spiritmythos.org/holy/ROA/sacsites/iona/ion_txt.html
13. https://snakespirit.webs.com/serpentsofiona.htm
14. https://www.esoterism.ro//english/island-druids.php
15. womanashealer.com/woman-shaman-2/about/
16. www.rahoorkhuit.net/goddess/ancient_priestesses/index.html
17. https://www.ancient-origins.net/history/female-druids-forgotten-priestesses-celts-005910
18. https://www.ancient-origins.net/history/female-druids-forgotten-priestesses-celts-005910
19. https://www.ancient-origins.net/history/female
20. https://en.wikipedia.org/wiki/Hildegard_of_Bingen
21. https://en.wikipedia.org//wiki/Asenath
22. http://www.aleph.se/Nada/Mage/Egypt/Priestesses.html
23. https://en.wikipedia.org/wiki/Hieros_gamos
24. https://orderwhitemoon.org/goddess/mary-virgin-mag/Magdalene.html
25. http://www.passageintopower.com/ /mary-magdalene-the-journey-of-the-sacred-priestess/
26. https://wiki2.org/en/Erythraean_Sibyl
27. https://www.scottishfield.co.uk/travel/scotland-travel/10-fascinating-facts-about-mull/

Chapter 8

The Labyrinths of Hades

Oracles of the Dead

The Oracle of the Dead at Baia, Italy, presided over by the Cumaean Sibyl (often mistaken for the Cimmerian Sibyl) is a labyrinth of cavernous tunnels carved out of volcanic rock barely passable for one person. It is a continuous descent downward into the bowels through an underground passage that leads one into the steamy hot earth. And as the patron pursuing answers would see, it was as if they descended into Hades itself all in an effort to hear their ancestors and receive the answers so desired. Travelling though one passageway after another one reached the River Styx (the principal river in the Greek Hades or underworld). Here was the border between the dead and the living. The ferryman took the seeker in his boat over the river transporting them to the cellar crypt where they would come face to face with the powerful writhing and mystical Oracle. What a visual! There she was seated in her box like tomb mouthing words for the Priest to interpret. Perhaps in a trance state because of the fissure cut into the earth and its escaping mesmerizing fumes.

Archaeologists have found five ruined buildings that sit against a steep volcanic hillside, in this ancient Roman site of Baia. Plus, above the terrace there was a discovery of more small rooms. This area was called "The Sacred Area" and was thought to be a beginning point in the ritual where patrons stopped before entering the tunnels buried deep in the hillside.

The Oracles and Sibyl's prophecies were never doubted and they were never questioned if the response was not what was expected. Some say these Priestesses only spoke in gibberish or disconnected phrases. But whatever words came forth they were very sought after and desired by seekers for centuries.

Many believe these ritual centers were sacred domiciles that contained portals to other realms that allowed the Priestesses to speak. Were these Priestesses, like many who practiced above ground, also affected by hallucinogenic substances in the form of vapors that leaked from deep underground crevices? That might explain the references to speaking in tongues. Those worthy patrons (Kings, Queens and the affluent) believed that their dignified status gave them the right to petition the Oracle. As they traversed through the labyrinth, they might also have felt the effects of vapors also. This could explain why they believed they were indeed traveling down to Hades where their ancestors awaited them with answers interpretated by an Oracle or Sibyl. The pure drama and spectacle of such an experience must have been life-changing. The petitioners believed deeply that the Oracles and Sibyls would bring them into contact with the Divine though their ancestors.

According to legend, she had the power of prophesy, and scribbled the future on oak leaves scattered at the entrance of her cave.[1]

The priests of the temple left nothing to chance and resorted to sending carrier pigeons to faraway lands to learn the fate of events (such as battles won and lost), so that they could appear more accurate in their interpretations of the priestess's vision.[2]

It was a hard life for these Priestesses who lived most of their lives underground in dark damp and toxic quarters. With the steady volume of generous patrons passing through the labyrinths these Priestesses were very profitable to the cave dwelling Priests. Constantly in deep trance to receive their messages from the dead must have been a contributing factor in their health and shortened life span. Did the extreme environment of this spiritual lifestyle create a continuous turnover of underground Sibyls?

There are other sites in ancient Italy where it is thought there were Oracles of the Dead structures. One is the site in the Phlegraean Fields of Campania, Italy. This site and others differ widely from deep cellar like crypts to catacomb tunnels and dark stone structures. As with many Oracles and Sibyls who went into trance to give their messages, these structures were also thought to sit upon fissures where toxic gases escaped. Some of these possibly emitted "mephitic" gases that would have influenced the conscious minds of the Sibyls who presided in these ancient cavities.

In the *Odyssey*, Odysseus is instructed by the Witch Circe how he can contact the dead. As the story continues Circe tells Odysseus to go to a specific cave and dig a shallow pit. He is then told to pour libations around it as a tribute to the dead. He is then told to pray. There is much more to this mythological story but I am fascinated by just how powerful the necessity was (and still is) to contact the dead whether in mythology or in reality. It is another example of just how powerful these ancient cave dwelling Oracles and Sibyls of the Dead were to the seekers who believed completely that they had the ability to channel their ancestors.

It was in the 1960's that the amateur archaeologist Robert Paget discovered the site at Baia. With Keith Jones, an American colleague and a number of volunteers he began an exploration of the antrum and after decade of excavating found a complex labyrinth like system of cavernous tunnels. Here was the "Cave of the Sibyl" as described by ancient authors. The underground Oracles who foretold the future deep within these earthy sacred rooms seemed to practice a more shadowy or mysterious side of prophecy.

In Hierapolis, Turkey, legend says that the Byzantine chapel of Aqioi Asomatoi was built on the vestiges of the Oracle of the

Dead with the Cave of Hades or Gate of Hades as the oracle entrance.

The Necromanteion

The Necromanteion was an ancient temple in Greece dedicated to Hades, the God of the Underworld, and his consort the Goddess Persephone. It was said to be located on the banks of the Acheron River in Epirus, near the ancient city of Ephyra. (Acheron was the son of the Goddess Gaia). The Temple Necromanteion of Acheron was so well known in the ancient world that believers are said to have flocked there by the thousands. The ancient Greeks imagined that souls were released from the decaying bodies of their ancestors buried deep in the earth. They believed the spirits of their dead travelled through the Underworld via cracks or crevices in the earth. To the ancient Greek societies these spirits had the power to foretell the future. This was the domain of the dead for the living did not possess these abilities. The belief continued and was centered around the otherworldly Oracles and Sibyls who sat upon these fissures in underground temples. For they had the power to communicate with the dead and receive their prophecies.

Although other ancient temples such as the Temple of Poseidon in Taenaron as well as those in Argolis, Cumae, and Herakleia in Pontos are known to have housed oracles of the dead, the Necromanteion of Ephyra was the most important.[3]

Endnotes:
1. https://eecarter.com/the-oracle-of-the-dead/
2. http://thehereticmagazine.com/oracles-of-the-dead/
3. https://en.wikipedia.org/wiki/Necromanteion_of_Acheron

Chapter 9

The Modern-Day Oracle Priestesses

There was always an abundance of seekers who wanted to know the outcome of their fortunes in the ancient world. This task was given to a group of select women who ancient societies trusted to unlock the mysteries of the unknown. There are voluminous historical accounts through the centuries where Emperors, Kings, Pharaohs, and Rulers all reached out for the prophetic words of female Oracles, Seers, and Sibyls. These ancient women were not only devoted Priestesses but deeply spiritually contemplative in their day to day lives. I am a Priestess who does trance meditation and I can attest to the enormous concentration that is needed to open the door to channel Deity. I have read accounts of ancient Priestesses dying from mental exhaustion after a particularly intense writhing session within deep trance. My ancestral sister Priestesses are a true inspiration. The celestial words of Deity that came through their mouths as they uttered their mystical messages influenced the integrity and character of ancient civilizations.

Sometimes their temple homes were simple structures, other times they were a complex series of buildings, like a city within a city. Archeological evidence about the role of the Temple Priestess is oftentimes controversial and always varied. Within the temple walls these very individual ancient Priestesses went into their unique trances to utter profound words of wisdom and prophetic guidance. Their words were not exclusively for the hierarchy, as many societies welcomed pilgrims who traveled far and for the opportunity to ask a question and receive an answer of an Oracle or Sibyl.

The tumultuous times of the ancient world is really not that dissimilar from our own world of chaotic political machinations and confusion. Today, Psychic advise has made a resurgence as modern societies try to make sense of all that is around them.

A modern Priestess can function quite well without living within a temple or cloister. We no longer need the protection of temple walls and in most modern societies we can live and work freely. The current Priestesses initiated within a number of wiccan and pagan traditions take their roles just as seriously as their predecessors, serving the spiritual needs of their covens and communities.

Traveling from antiquity to the present I have traced the threads of many unique and interesting stories of powerful spiritual women. Today we not only have Priestesses, but many authors, teachers, oracles, psychics. Mediums and sacred dancers. In many current societies, women have more freedom to pursue their psychic vocations and follow in the footsteps of their ancestors. As in the past, history often paints these ancient women as less significant. The mystical sciences are mysterious and many fear what they don't understand. Our primordial sisters, Priestess pioneers of the ancient world, have inspired and stirred the soul of every modern Priestess as we continue the sacred journey.

Helena Petrovna Blavatsky

Helena Petrovna Blavatsky (known as Madam Blavatsky) was born on August 12, 1831 and passed away on May 8, 1891. She was a Russian philosopher and author who co-founded the Theosophical Society in 1875. She was well known as a leading theoretician of theosophy. At a very early age she developed an interest in Western esotericism and in her later years she traveled extensively throughout the world. Madam Blavatsky was someone who was fascinated to discover and experience diverse spiritual and mystical practices. She claimed to channel a group of spiritual adepts whom she called the "Masters of the Ancient Wisdom". Heavily involved in the spiritualist movement she moved to New Yok City in 1873 and rose to public attention as a spirit medium. In 1875 she co-founded the Theosophical Society with Henry Steel Olcott. Theosophy is tied to the esoteric doctrines of Hermeticism and Neoplatonism.

Blavatsky described Theosophy as "the synthesis of science, religion and philosophy", proclaiming that it was reviving an "Ancient Wisdom" which underlay all the world's religions.[1]

A brilliantly vibrant personality, Madam Blavatsky, had her share of critics. But she remains one of the most mysterious free thinkers and influential spiritualists of her day. She was the author of *Isis Unveiled: A Master-Key to the Mysteries of Ancient and Modern Science and Theology*; *The Secret Doctrine: The Synthesis of Science, Religion, and Philosophy*; and *The Voice of the Silence*.

As a devout matriarch of the Divine Feminine and dedicated spirit medium she joined her ancient sisters in channeling mystical messages from the Elysian.

Jeane Dixon

Jeane Dixon (January 5, 1904 – January 25, 1997) was one of the most famous psychics and astrologers in the twentieth century. She was born Lydia Pinckert in 1904. According to legend during her youth in California, Jeane received a crystal ball from a gypsy who predicted she would become a famous psychic and "advise powerful people" throughout the world.

Dixon's most famous prediction was the assassination of President John F. Kennedy, which she wrote about in 1956, seven years before it happened. Dixon went on to write several successful books and a regular newspaper column. The gypsy's prediction also came true — in 1971, Dixon advised president Richard Nixon on possible terrorist attacks in America.

Doreen Valiente

Doreen Valiente (January 4, 1922 – September 1, 1999) was an Englishwomen who was initiated in 1953 by Gerald Gardner into a tradition of Witchcraft. Soon afterwards she was the High Priestess of Gerald Gardner's "Bricket Wood Coven" and she is thought to be responsible for much of the early Gardnerian liturgy. As an author and poet, she adapted many ancient texts into what became known as "The Witches Rune" and "The Charge of the Goddess". Both became incorporated into the *Gardnerian Book of Shadows*. She also published numerous books dealing with esoteric subjects in addition to Witchcraft.

As a Priestess she was interested in the early research of her religion's history and became involved in the Witchcraft Research Association. As an author she contributed to the published works of her Wiccan friends Stewart and Janet Farrar. In her later years she served as a patron of the Sussex-based Centre for Pagan Studies.

As a modern-day Priestess and Oracle, she channeled Divinity in writings that have inspired Witches and Wiccans for decades.

Within the occult community, Valiente has become internationally known as the "Mother of Modern Witchcraft" or "Mother of Wica", although she herself disliked this moniker.[2]

Sybil Leek

Sybil Leek was an English Witch, astrologer, occult author and psychic, who was born on February 22, 1917 and died on October 26, 1982. She was the author of over 60 books and numerous magazine articles on all subjects of the occult including astrology and various other esoteric subjects. Her autobiography *Diary of a Witch*, was a declaration that Witchcraft was not dead and was still very much alive. Because of the popularity of her book, the BBC labelled her "Britian's most famous Witch". From that time onward she attracted a lot of public attention. She was harassed by landlords and the public who felt a genuine prejudice against Witches. In her diary she writes about living with the Romany Gypsies in the New Forest where she learned about ancient folklore and the practical use of herbs. She then went on to become, for a short time, the High Priestess of the Horsa Coven also in the New Forest. At one point she was invited to New York by a publisher and there she met Hans Holzer a parapsychologist who was investigating psychic phenomena. They were a creditable team and produced many television and radio programs on their investigations. She was the medium Hans trusted most in his ground breaking research of the paranormal. Sybil was a trance medium which meant she was able to pass on (channel) messages from the deceased while in a state of deep trance. Trance mediums are also called oracles. Eventually she toured and lectured frequently in the US, England and Europe. She made a lasting mark on the Witchcraft community and that of real psychics and mediums.

Much has been written about Sybil Leek, most of it controversial as many did not agree with her beliefs or her methods. As with our ancient Priestesses whose stories were so often eliminated from ancient texts, I believe Sybil was not given her due. She was active in the repeal of Britian's Witchcraft Act in 1951 which then gave her a safe platform to not only practice but write about the ancient traditions of the craft.

Her legacy will live on. (Her books have achieved cult status and are very expensive and often difficult to obtain).

A coven of white witches in the New Forest are following in Sybil's footsteps. High Priestess Julie Forest says: "She was a pioneer of her time and she is an inspiration to modern day witches."[3]

Lady Olivia Robertson

Olivia Melian Robertson was born on Friday, April 13th, 1917 and passed into the spirit world on November 14, 2013. Olivia was a healer and in 1940 she served as a V.A.D. nurse in Berkshire during WWII and in the 1960's along with her brother Lawrence and his wife Pamela ran a local welfare system. She was also a successful artist and writer who authored a number of books including *Field of the Stranger* that was named Book Society Choice in London.

Later in the 1960's she moved back to her ancestral home of Clonegal Castle with her brother Lawrence and his wife. There the three formed the Huntington Castle Centre for Meditation and Study. Olivia had a talent for guiding others in meditation or "magical journeys" as she called them. Beginning a journey of self-discovery she investigated Christianity, Theosophy, Hinduism and Sufism.

As her awareness of the Goddesses deepened, she realized the Goddess embodied the Divine Chalice, the Holy Grail. As a symbol of the Divine Feminine Principle, it began to have a transformative effect upon her life.[4]

Along with her brother and sister-in-law they continued to work with psychism and each had wonderful visions of the Goddess, which eventually led to their forming of the Fellowship of Isis (FOI). Olivia as an Oracle Priestess of Isis traveled extensively throughout Europe and the USA. As a trance medium she provided oracular messages and her sacred liturgy awakened the essence of the Divine Feminine in rituals honoring the Goddess. The Fellowship of Isis liturgy that she wrote has a worldwide audience.

A true Temple Priestess of the Goddess, Olivia was also a Sacred Dancer. As a dancer and teacher of Sacred dance and a Priestess within the FOI, I had the great pleasure to know Lady

Olivia quite well. Once I gave her the gift of a "dancers chiffon tunic" which she immediately wore. Olivia danced each step that I taught and my dearest memory was of her looking down at my feet and copying so very carefully my every nuance and expression. She would then dance and let her spirit soar with inspiration and abandon.

And on the day of her passing in 2013, the faeries made her one of them and away they danced into the night.

Laurie Cabot, HPS

Laurie was born on March 6, 1933 and was one of the first people to popularize Witchcraft in the United States and is the author of several books. She founded the Cabot Tradition of Witchcraft and the Cabot Kent Hermetic Temple, a non-profit Wiccan Church. She also founded The Witches' League for Public Awareness to defend the civil rights of Witches everywhere. She is a long-time member of the Fellowship of Isis and was a friend to Lady Olivia Robetson. Laurie is a force to be reckoned with. In the 1970's she was declared the "Official Witch of Salem, Massachusetts" by Governor Michael Dukakis to honor her work with special children. Laurie still resides in Salem, Massachusetts and is part of Salem lore. She has been in many documentaries and talk shows and has been interviewed for numerous periodicals. She is the author of a number of books and is definitely the most recognized Witch in the World. She follows in the footsteps of the Temple Priestesses of Antiquity, her ancestral sisters.

I have witnessed her as an Oracle and in her trance medium states she is truly gifted as she channels the Goddess illuminating the Divine. She is also a Sacred Dancer as well as a talented artist. We have danced together in ceremonial rituals and her flowing grace has always melded with mine to raise worshipful energy in honor of the Goddess.

She has been a dear friend and almost a mother, for most of my adult life. During the years we have shared many adventures (which could be a book in itself!). Observers have said that when we are together there is an aura and vibration that passes from one to the other. Those who are intuitive can feel the sacrosanct between us.

Lady Belladonna Laveau, HPS

Lady Belladonna Laveau is the Archpriestess and Matriarch of the Aquarian Tabernacle Church International (ATC) and the dean of Woolston-Steen Theological Seminary, an EDU. The Seminary is the only recognized Wiccan sponsored college in the United States. Bella is a true Temple Priestess and Sacred Dancer who lives within the Mother Church/Temple. She is considered one of the leading voices of the Goddess in the Witchcraft and pagan communities as she serves a modern congregation. She is a Sibyl and Hierophant of the Great Mother Goddess Demeter. With her intuitive oracular spirit Bella is a direct channel to the Goddess and serves at her behest. She is a sister Priestess and it is with her encouragement that I joined the faculty of Woolston-Steen Theological Seminary. In 2019 on Gallows Hill in Salem, Massachusetts, three High Priestesses; Bella, Gypsy Ravish and myself channeled the "Three Fates" during our Samhain Ritual not knowing how very appropriate their wise words would be.

Gypsy Ravish, HPS

Gypsy Ravish is the High Priestess of the Coven of Akhelarre in Salem, Massachusetts, in the Alexandrian Traditional Lineage family of Wicca. She is also the principal Minister of the Temple of Nine Wells, ATC in Salem whose congregation presents public Rituals for all the Wiccan Sabbats. The Temple of Nine Well is an affiliate of The Aquarian Tabernacle Church. Gypsy is a singer/songwriter whose music came to her through dreams and invocations from life challenges, deep tribal memories and connections to the Ancestors. In processional ceremonies her music encircles the participants in light. She too is a true Temple Priestess.

Lady Haight- Ashton, HPS – Oracle, Sibyl and Sacred Dancer

Lady Haight-Ashton is a modern Temple Priestess. She is an author, teacher, Sacred Dancer, and a Priestess of Lilith, Selket, Hecate and Isis. She is the High Priestess of Sacred Moon Coven, affiliated with The Aquarian Tabernacle Church (ATC), and the High Priestess of the Iseum of the Graceful Goddess and a Priestess in the Fellowship of Isis (FOI). Lady is a professional psychic medium with clients in the USA and Canada, licensed Clergy Counselor, member of the Maine Pagan Clergy Association, the Crossroads Lyceum and the Sacred Dance Guild. She is the author of numerous books including *The First Sisters: Lilith and Eve* and this book.

A psychic since childhood, Lady now practices within a trance medium state, where she periodically transcends this dimension blending the spirit world with the physical. In her altered state of consciousness, she records her verbal and written oracular messages from the Goddess to share with her fellow Witches and Psychics (and the public) in rituals.

Lily Dale Assembly in Lily Dale, NY (a town of mediums)

When Lily Dale was founded 140 years ago, it was created as a place unlike any other. Not for being flashy or grand, as much of what is different about Lily Dale is not visible. This is a place people come to renew, to expand, to connect, to explore. Mediumship - talking to the dead - has been an important part of Lily Dale since the very beginning, but what many people don't know is how much healing has played a role in the creation and evolution of the place. In the early days this included critical social justice movements of the time, in particular women's suffrage, as well as early developments of alternative healing from the laying on of hands to hypnosis.

Lily Dale is an international member organization and residential community comprised of persons who practice the faith of Spiritualism, which is an active faith guided by a set of principles. This faith is applied through prayer, meditation, healing, and mediumship.

Lily Dale is a year-round community, that is home to more than 50 professionally registered mediums. It is also the home of a thriving community of Spiritualists, including groups and committees dedicated to every aspect of running a summer program and year-round activities for residents and visitors alike.

Endnotes:

1. https://en.wikipedia.org//wiki/Helena_Blavatsky
2. https://en.wikipedia.org//wiki/Doreen_Valiente
3. http://www.bbc.co.uk/insideout/south/series1/sybil-leek.shtml
4. https://www.fellowshipofisiscentral.com/fellowship-of-isis---biographies-of-the-founders

Chapter 10

The Oracle Messages

The Sibylline Oracles

The Sibylline Oracles (Latin: Oracular Sibyllina; sometimes called the pseudo-Sibylline Oracles) are a collection of oracular utterances written in Greek hexameters ascribed to the Sibyls, prophets who uttered divine revelations in a frenzied state.[1]

The Sibyls were the oracles of ancient Greece and according to legends, similar throughout antiquity, prophesied at holy sites (temples).

Their prophecies were influenced by divine inspiration from a deity; originally at Delphi and Pessinos. In Late Antiquity, various writers attested to the existence of sibyls in Greece, Italy, the Levant, and Asia Minor.[2]

Only fourteen books and eight fragments of the ancient Greek Sibylline Oracles have survived in an edition that was printed in the 6th or 7th century CE. Regretfully, the original Sibylline Books of oracular texts from the ancient Tuscans and Romans were burned by order of the Roman Flavius Stilicho in the 4th century CE. I have read the Sibylline Oracles and I agree with many other historians and herstorians that in their existing form they are a bit chaotic but definitely interpretative and meaningful. Of unknown authorship with mixed religious beliefs, they are like a medley of fragmented phrases and words. The Oracles are housed within hexameter verses with a diverse character referencing royalty, temples, kingdoms and various people. There is a definite mystery surrounding the Sibylline Oracles. Are books 3-5 really the oldest and as legend records partly composed by Alexandrian Jews; were books 1-2 written or recorded by Christians? I chose to follow herstory and my belief that the fragmented phrases within these books were actually spoken by ancient Sibyls and Oracles, whoever recorded them. Whatever the controversary, there is value in these ancient words.

Milton Terry (1840-1914) was a Professor of Hebrew, Old Testament exegesis and Theology. He has translated a version of the Oracles that seems to have been privately printed for there is no publisher listed. Here is an excerpt from the beginning in 1. Book 1.
Beginning with the generation first
Of mortal men down to the very last
I'll prophecy each thing: what erst has been
And what is now, and what shall yet befall.

The Catholic Encyclopedia states, "Through the decline and disappearance of paganism, however, interest in them gradually diminished and they ceased to be widely read or circulated, though they were known and used during the Middle Ages in both the East and the West."[3]

Plutarch on the Cessation of Oracles
Plutarch was a Greek philosopher, historian, biographer and essayist. He spent the last decades of his life as a Priest at the Temple of Apollo and thus had first-hand knowledge of the lives of the Pythia Priestesses. *On the Cessation of Oracles* is a collection of memories in essay format with an occasional phrase from a Pythia. But his work can be summed up in this verse:

Plutarch's answer to the question why many oracles in Greece have ceased to function is that the population is now much less than it was, and so there is less need for oracles now than in earlier times.[4]

Endnotes:

1. https://en.wikipedia.org/wiki/Sibylline_Oracles
2. https://en.wikipedia.org/wiki/Sibyl
3. https://en.wikipedia.org/wiki/Sibylline_Oracles
4. www.perseus.tufts.edu/hopper/text?doc=Perseus:text:2008.01.0251

Oracles of Lady Haight-Ashton

I am an Oracle draped in a gossamer veil who can descend into trance meditation. I can communicate between the spirits of the dead and the living. Following in the footsteps of my ancient Oracle and Sibyl ancestors, I also channel Divinity. Each Sabbat I allow myself to go into a trance meditative state and receive an Oracle message. I have included many of these Sabbat messages in this book starting with the important Samhain of 2019.

In October of 2019 I received numerous messages that revolved around the "three fates" and the fate of the world. At that time no one fully grasped that the pandemic would have such a devastating outcome. Here is a sequence of events that was played out in Salem, Massachusetts (with my oracle messages and visions) during our Samhain Ritual on Gallows Hill. Three witches joined in channeling the fates and weaving a spell of awakening. For I believe I was given a message that as a society we needed to be awakened to the dangers that lay ahead and with that information we could protect ourselves.

Oracle given in October 2019 - Samhain Ritual on Gallows Hill, Salem, Massachusetts

Three veiled Priestesses/Witches moving/dancing around a cauldron fire near the Altar. saying these words three times:

We conjure thee O Fates of three
Mistresses of Destiny, Fortune and Chance
Spinners, weavers and cutters of thread
Priestesses three, our time has come
As old things die and blow away
The New Year dawns - so mote this Spell
Let shadows fade and light shine through
For a better future and peaceful today
For all of humanity and the world
Earth, Air, Fire, Water and Spirit
Bring to us the outcome we desire
As born by three - we invoke the eternal harmony
This is our will – So Mote It Be

Three Priestesses take the cords and together braid the Spell -

one begins to braid while another reads this - three times:

Braiding the Cords
Over, under, weave the threads of Fate
As in life, so in all things
By the powers of old our Magick grows
Nimble hands intertwine our cords
Weave the pattern of Awakening
By the power of Three Times Three
As we will it, So Mote It Be

And finally, an Invocation spoken by all three:

Invocation to the Three Fates
O Lady with the spindle
Weave my destiny
Spin the thread of my beginning
Weave the truth of my spirit
O Lady with the shuttle
Let the shuttle work back and forth
Creating the tapestry of my life
Whose threads become my strength
O Lady with the shears
Whose wise hand is my fate
And likewise, my truth.

Oracle given for the Samhain Ritual, October 31, 2020
I am Lilith the Goddess of Wild Freedom...I am the Goddess of Death and Transformation. Listen to the words of the Oracle. Be generous to your fellow humans, animals and all creatures. A candle flame is not lessoned when light is taken from it to light many candles. Share your light and love with all and you will gain all.

Oracle given for the Yule/Winter Solstice Ritual, December 221, 020

I call forth the voice of the Sacred Oracle...allow Her Divine words to resound through our mortal beings...welcome contemplation and reflection. The purpose shall bring the prospect of expectation.

Let our hearts seek the hallowed pathway that will bring us to the purest essence of the Goddess and God. The ancient wheel turns, light returns. What will be is now. What was will coexist with all that is of this day and age. The world has wept through glistening tears for too long. Wipe them away and let the shadows fade...let the sunshine glow with yellows, oranges and the vibrant reds of passion and all life.

Oracle given on for the Imbolc/Candlemas Ritual, February 2, 2021

The Oracle speaks
Holy Mother Brid calls to us with Her chorus
As the mighty winds of change blow; the oceans, rivers and streams begin to tremble
Everything pours into the Center
The Sacred Well shall surge until the rhythm of water becomes audible
All rise to the reverberation of the harmony
Witness the flowing waters of holy source
The consecrated shall sustain all
Behold the gentle silence of the Universe that will envelope all things
As dust vanishes, brightness begins to glimmer
Observe! The Wheel of Destiny turns yet again
Dismiss all arrogance and injustice
Let honor and tolerance prevail
For with pure reverence, we shall never want
Ah! we are all supplicants to Divinity

Oracle given on for the Ostara/Spring Equinox Ritual, March 20, 2021

Harken to the voice of the Oracle, for her words shall "Lift the Veil". She speaks softly in unison within the etheric essence of the unknown that surrounds us. Listen to her, for the Goddess speaks through her and she will transport you to an initiation of realization.

Feel the persona of the Empress who becomes the expansive Sophia transporting us through the Cosmos into our physical world. She allows us to become open enough to receive, to melt into a surrendered state of soothing exchange. Reach for the tender Yin flow. The Emperor's persona is collective as the universe smiles and the Yang merges with the Yin. He holds court at the throne of the Goddess. Here we have the subtle duality of the Cosmos that connects us to the new cycle of our physical earth.

Arouse yourself from your worldly slumber to become an open channel by which the spirit of the Goddess can be heard within you. Dissolve into a state of perceptive understanding.

Take heed, for the Oracle is wise...from the stirred tears of her soul to yours let the Divine essence of transcendence fill you, as you fill others with hope. Move tenderly into the gentle relaxation of euphoria, as you enter into the spacious aura of the Goddess. There is only unconditional love in an accessible and receptive heart.

Oracle given on Beltaine/May Day, May 1, 2021

I call forth the voice of the Sacred Oracle...allow Her Divine words to resound through our mortal beings.

Sophia, Goddess of Divine contradiction. She is the Celestial seed of spirituality in a material world. Within her myth lies her ancient wisdom. Through her we can find the missing part of our understanding. Our journey is to cultivate compassion. If we open up to the existence of suffering only then can we aspire to its healing. Empathy becomes our strength, kindness becomes our courage, tolerance becomes equality. There is joy in being human even in loss and separation. Honor yourself while you seek the essence of exploration within your being.

The wheel turns yet again and the natural world transcends into the ethereal dimensions of the mystical. The incandescence rays of the Sun blaze forth into the luminous fires of Beltaine. The realm of the Faerie folk beckons us to join in their ravenous dancing and celebration. Colorful ribbons mimicking our destinies intertwine around the phallic Maypole. Goddess and God fertility abounds within the sacred bonfires where the mysteries of life, death and rebirth lay hidden in flames. Rejoice in your life, your future and all that destiny will show you.

Oracle given on Litha/Summer Solstice Ritual, June 20, 2021

Let the voice of the Oracle be heard. We are surrounded by shadows. Hidden within our unconscious mind is the light where the realm of wholeness within our soul fulfills our highest purpose. But first we must descend into the darkness, where all things are hidden. Draw aside the Veil to see the path that leads to the Temple of the Sun. Follow the cavernous path that leads you to the gate that can only be opened with the key of destiny. Summon your heart to true wakefulness.

Rise up and walk forward into the light of the eternal dawn to see the Goddess who wears the solar crown. From her the brilliant radiance of the rainbow's rays spirals down upon us. She is the life-seed of the Great Mother who holds the plump seeds of life that will reach the air and the sky.

Oracle given on Lughnasadh/Lammas Celebration, August 1, 2021

Hail the Oracle speaks. Blessings bestowed upon the great Goddess Tailtiu whose scythe sheaves the grain as she perishes from exhaustion. The Wheel of Life spins around once again. Let us bless this abundance, let us bless the grain that is the life blood of civilization in her honor.

Feed your shadow with this abundance so that you may feel your physical body. Touch your physical self as you remember that you are a part of the eternal life of the earth. Become aware of the radiance of your body of light. Open your heart to those in need. If you truly achieve love, you can awaken all of your senses. Your shadow shall turn to light and will be reflected in the sphere of Divinity. You are part of the cosmic whole as the spiritual milk of life runs through your veins. Build the transcendent essence within your soul and reflect upon your mortality.

References

Iris J. Stewart, 2013, Sacred *Woman, Sacred Dance,* Inner Traditions.

Jorge Guillermo, 2013, *Sibyls Prophecy and Power in the Ancient World,* Overlook Duckworth, Peter Mayers Publishers Inc.

https://findanyanswer.com/What were the duties of priests in Sumerian society?

https://isiopolis.com/2013/04/06/women-as-priests-in-ancient-egypt/

https://en.wikipedia.org/wiki/Temple_of_Isis_(Pompeii)

https://www.ancient.eu//article/680/daily-life-in-ancient-mesopotamia/

http://www.aleph.se/Nada/Mage/Egypt/Priestesses.html

https://www.ancient-origins.net/history/history/serpent-priestesses-and-ancient-sexual-rites.

https://www.atlasobscura.com//articles/the-medieval-prophetess-who-used-her-visions-to-criticize-the-church

https://ritualgoddess.compriestess-diviners-of-minoan-crete/priestess-diviners-of-minoan-crete/

https://en.wikipedia.org/wiki/Minoan_religion

https://www.ancient-origins.net/myths-legends/tattooed-priestesses-hathor-001122

https://www.ancient.eu/article/74/the-women-of-athenas-cult/

https://www.historicmysteries.com/oracle-of-delphi-pythia/

https://www.travelfranceonline.com/ile-de-sein-raz-de-sein-finistere/https://www.goddess-pages.co.uk/goddess-nine-maidens/

http://suppressedhistories.net/articles/priestesses.html

https://www.themystica.com/shamanism/

https://www.esotcrism.ro//english/island-druids.php

https://en.wikipedia.org/wiki/Hypatia

https://historica.fandom.com/wiki/Chrysis

https://www.worldhistory.org/article/32/the-eleusinian-mysteries-the-rites-of-demeter/

https://www.ancient.eu/timeline/Greek_Culture/

https://www.ancient-origins.net/history/female-druids-
forgotten-priestesses-celts-005910

www.spiritmythos.org/holy/ROA/sacsites/iona/ion_txt.html

https://en.wikipedia.org/wiki/Hildegard_of_Bingen

https://www.newworldencyclopedia.org/ /entry/Ishtar

https://en.wikipedia.org/wiki/Iset_(priestess)

http://www.passageintopower.com/   http://mary-magdalene-
the-journey-of-the-sacred-priestess/

https://orderwhitemoon.org/goddess/mary-virgin-mag/
Magdalene.html

https://oracleofthedead.com

https://oracleofthedead.com/an-oracle-at-baia/

https://www.ancient-origins.net/   news-myths-legends/
necromanteion-ancient-temple-dead

https://www.atlasobscura.com/places/st-brigid-s-well

https://thewitchesalmanac.com//sybil-leek/

https://en.wikipedia.org/wiki/Mother_Shipton

https://en.wikipedia.org/wiki/North_Berwick_witch_trials

You may also be interested in

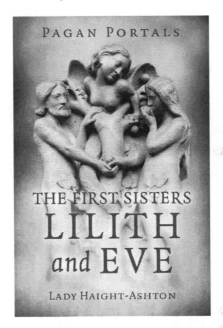

The First Sisters: Lilith and Eve
Lady Haight-Ashton

*The tale of Lilith, the first female, so troublesome she was
Erased from mythology to be replaced by her sister, Eve.*

978-1-78904-079-1 (Paperback)
978-1-78904-080-7 (ebook)

MOON
BOOKS

PAGANISM & SHAMANISM

What is Paganism? A religion, a spirituality, an alternative belief system, nature worship? You can find support for all these definitions (and many more) in dictionaries, encyclopaedias, and text books of religion, but subscribe to any one and the truth will evade you. Above all Paganism is a creative pursuit, an encounter with reality, an exploration of meaning and an expression of the soul. Druids, Heathens, Wiccans and others, all contribute their insights and literary riches to the Pagan tradition. Moon Books invites you to begin or to deepen your own encounter, right here, right now.

If you have enjoyed this book, why not tell other readers by posting a review on your preferred book site.

Recent bestsellers from Moon Books are:

Journey to the Dark Goddess
How to Return to Your Soul
Jane Meredith
Discover the powerful secrets of the Dark Goddess and
transform your depression, grief and pain into healing
and integration.
Paperback: 978-1-84694-677-6 ebook: 978-1-78099-223-5

Shamanic Reiki
Expanded Ways of Working with Universal Life Force Energy
Llyn Roberts, Robert Levy
Shamanism and Reiki are each powerful ways of healing; together,
their power multiplies. *Shamanic Reiki* introduces techniques to
help healers and Reiki practitioners tap ancient healing wisdom.
Paperback: 978-1-84694-037-8 ebook: 978-1-84694-650-9

Pagan Portals – The Awen Alone
Walking the Path of the Solitary Druid
Joanna van der Hoeven
An introductory guide for the solitary Druid, *The Awen Alone* will
accompany you as you explore, and seek out your own place
within the natural world.
Paperback: 978-1-78279-547-6 ebook: 978-1-78279-546-9

A Kitchen Witch's World of Magical Herbs & Plants
Rachel Patterson
A journey into the magical world of herbs and plants, filled with
magical uses, folklore, history and practical magic. By popular
writer, blogger and kitchen witch, Tansy Firedragon.
Paperback: 978-1-78279-621-3 ebook: 978-1-78279-620-6

Medicine for the Soul
The Complete Book of Shamanic Healing
Ross Heaven
All you will ever need to know about shamanic healing and how to
become your own shaman…
Paperback: 978-1-78099-419-2 ebook: 978-1-78099-420-8

Shaman Pathways – The Druid Shaman
Exploring the Celtic Otherworld
Danu Forest
A practical guide to Celtic shamanism with exercises and
techniques as well as traditional lore for exploring the Celtic
Otherworld.
Paperback: 978-1-78099-615-8 ebook: 978-1-78099-616-5

Traditional Witchcraft for the Woods and Forests
A Witch's Guide to the Woodland with Guided Meditations and
Pathworking
Mélusine Draco
A Witch's guide to walking alone in the woods, with guided
meditations and pathworking.
Paperback: 978-1-84694-803-9 ebook: 978-1-84694-804-6

Wild Earth, Wild Soul
A Manual for an Ecstatic Culture
Bill Pfeiffer
Imagine a nature-based culture so alive and so connected,
spreading like wildfire. This book is the first flame…
Paperback: 978-1-78099-187-0 ebook: 978-1-78099-188-7

Naming the Goddess
Trevor Greenfield
Naming the Goddess is written by over eighty adherents and
scholars of Goddess and Goddess Spirituality.
Paperback: 978-1-78279-476-9 ebook: 978-1-78279-475-2

Shapeshifting into Higher Consciousness
Heal and Transform Yourself and Our World with Ancient
Shamanic and Modern Methods
Llyn Roberts
Ancient and modern methods that you can use every day to
transform yourself and make a positive difference in the world.
Paperback: 978-1-84694-843-5 ebook: 978-1-84694-844-2

Readers of ebooks can buy or view any of these bestsellers by
clicking on the live link in the title. Most titles are published in
paperback and as an ebook. Paperbacks are available in traditional
bookshops. Both print and ebook formats are available online.

Find more titles and sign up to our readers' newsletter at
http://www.johnhuntpublishing.com/paganism
Follow us on Facebook at https://www.facebook.com/MoonBooks
and Twitter at https://twitter.com/MoonBooksJHP